"Dr. Richards has done magnificently well in approaching the problems that divide us. . . . For the most part, we all have far more in common than we have in basic differences.

"It is my prayer that the volume will have an increasing audience. . . . It is a privilege for me to commend the volume to the reading, thinking public."

W. A. Criswell

"With complete respect for the great foundational truths of Scripture which are unalterable, the author gives clear guidelines for believers who otherwise hold some differing views on other matters but desire 'to keep the unity of the Spirit in the bond of peace.' "

—Paul Van Gorder, **The Radio Bible Class** and TV's **Day of Discovery**

LARRY RICHARDS holds a B.A. in philosophy from the University of Michigan, where he was graduated magna cum laude and elected to Phi Beta Kappa. He graduated with honor from Dallas Theological Seminary, and received the Ph.D. degree from Northwestern University. He now lives in Phoenix, Arizona, where he directs the activities of Renewal Research Associates, a not-for-profit public foundation dedicated to the vitalization of the local church. His books include Creative Bible Teaching, Creative Bible Study, A New Face for the Church, *and* Science and the Bible: Can Both Be Right?

BECOMING ONE
IN THE SPIRIT

LARRY RICHARDS

Published by
VICTOR BOOKS

a division of SP Publications, Inc.
Wheaton, Illinois 60187

Scripture references in this book are quoted by permission
from *The Modern Language Bible*, the Berkeley Version,
© 1945, 1959, 1969 by the Zondervan Publishing House,
unless otherwise noted. Other versions quoted are identified
as follows:

   AV—the Authorized Version (King James)
   PH—The New Testament in Modern English, © 1958,
      J.B. Phillips (by permission of Macmillan)
   LB—The Living Bible paraphrase by Kenneth Taylor
      (by permission of Tyndale)

BECOMING ONE IN THE SPIRIT

Published by Victor Books, a Division of SP Publications, Inc.

Third printing January, 1975

ISBN: 0-88207-235-8

Printed in the United States of America

VICTOR BOOKS
A Division of SP Publications, Inc.,
Wheaton, Illinois 60187, U.S.A.

Contents

Introduction

A Note

This book explores the Bible's teaching on Christian unity and develops biblical principles that show us how to experience unity. But it is not just a book to read . . . it invites you to experience God's truth.

To help you apply and experience the concepts explored, read the book, if possible, with other people. A *Leader's Guide** that suggests a variety of things to talk over and do with others is available. You can use this book and the guide with as few as two—a husband and wife, perhaps—as a study for a church board, in a Sunday School class, or a home Bible study.

The Bible's teaching on becoming one in the Spirit is meant to guide us in our relationships with others in Christ's Church. So study it with others . . . and together seek God the Holy Spirit's help to build unity within the body of Christ.

LARRY RICHARDS

*For 95¢ at your local bookstore or from Scripture Press, Wheaton, Ill. 60187.

1

Created One

This book is about what is, and yet isn't. About a oneness in the Spirit that God says He has created (it therefore is), but a oneness that Christians must maintain (it may slip away from us and not be experienced).

It's so easy for oneness to be lost. In nearly every important relationship. . . .

(1)

Carl stood still for a moment, then turned and fumbled for the evening newspaper. He hated it—this feeling of frustration and guilt that left him so helpless. *God knows I've tried*, he thought. But somehow his trying was never enough. He'd failed Ellen . . . and both of them knew it. Now, when he tried to reach out to her, or promised a new start in their infrequent family devotions, her lips just tightened. And the guilt and frustration swelled up in him.

Carl scanned the sports headlines, still thinking of the way his and Ellen's marriage had worked out. They'd just have to be satisfied with the home and marriage they had now. A good home. A good marriage. One where there was a fair measure of love, and companionship, and shared churchgoing. But a marriage that fell short of what both he and Ellen had looked for when they married. One that fell short of the oneness and joy and harmony that the Bible seems to hold out as a promise to those who not only become one in the marriage relationship but also share oneness in Christ.

Carl and Ellen had reached out to each other, had known a growing love . . . but also a growing frustration as the oneness they yearned for seemed to escape them.

Looking up, Carl cleared his throat. "I see the Giants are only one game out. But I think the Reds will catch them pretty soon. They're pretty hot right now."

Ellen smiled and nodded.

And life settled down again into its familiar routine.

(2)

Scene: The church board room, with meeting in progress.

VIC (*showing irritation as he looks around the table at which eight men are seated*): "The board has talked about Ed and Carrie a dozen times, and we can't agree. I think we just have to leave it to the Lord, and get on. . . ."

BILL (*interrupting*): "As leaders of this church, we're responsible to take care of God's flock. Carrie's really hurting, Vic, and we all know that Ed's seeing Susan Phelps. There are two families that are going to be destroyed, and five kids that are. . . ."

GEORGE (*calm and reasonable*): "All right, Bill,

10

we all know that. But there's no question of adultery yet. Ed's still in the church—still sings in the choir. And you know he denies anything wrong when anyone tries to talk with him."

BILL *(heatedly)*: "Come off it, George. Ed's told Carrie he plans to get a divorce."

GEORGE *(soothing)*: "Sure, but he hasn't done it yet, has he? So what can we do? If it were a case of open sin, we'd have some biblical guidelines. . . ."

LES *(angry)*: "Come off it, George. You know some of us feel we've got enough scriptural guidance . . . and that the rest of you are simply afraid to act on it!"

At this point, half a dozen angry voices are heard:

"Now just a minute . . . !"

"You know we've got to act . . . !"

"Of all the hypocritical . . . !"

VIC *(pounding the table with gavel, shouting over the clamor of voices)*: "That's all! That's all! Meeting's over for tonight.

"Go home . . . and don't bring this up again here. We'll meet tomorrow night to take care of our business. And when we do, for God's sake, let's try to work *together!*"

(3)

Scene: Outside church after a morning service. Main Character: A young "Jesus person" really trying to make it in the established church. *What does he hear?*

"That was a fine sermon, Pastor."

"Thank you, Brother Reddick."

11

"Really enjoyed it today, Pastor."

"It was good to see you out again Auntie May."

"Morning, Pastor."

And what does he think?

Do they really mean it? What goes on behind the masks, the Sunday clothes and ties, the neat, short haircuts?

It's really weird. I mean, sitting there in that church with a bunch of strangers. Strangers who look away from me, pretending not to see my long hair (it's neat, isn't it, tied back in a club behind my scrubbed face and neatly trimmed beard?). It's really weird. Here they are, Christians like me, all lined up in quiet rows, sitting side by side, but I can't see inside them. I don't know them, and they don't know me. And they don't want to know me, either.

I mean, I can take it. I'm used to it. And I've got fellowship, real fellowship, with some of the other Jesus people. But . . . , man, it's just weird.

All lined up.

So quiet.

Smiling and shaking hands.

I guess it's all right if they don't want to know me. But I wonder. Do they even know each other? Does anybody reach out? Does anyone really care about what's going on inside another person here? Or is it really like what I feel?

Just a gathering of strangers.

Just rows and rows of dressed up bodies.

But no love.

Man, I don't want to preach, but when Jesus

says you know His disciples by their love for each
other, I've gotta go along with Him. All the way.

And I don't feel any love there.

I wonder if they feel any?

(4)

"And then we started talking with this couple at lunch. They were very nice and all. We found out they go to church, that funny church over on the other side of town. So we started talking about what they believe.

"Well, they believe like us in a lot of things, but there are some big differences. They think you have to go to their church to be saved, for one thing. When they found out we are Presbyterians, you could see that they thought we were in trouble with the Lord! And they believe that a Christian can be lost after he's saved; we talked about that for a while, too.

"They were a real nice couple, but though we talked about what we each believe, we never got to know each other as persons. You know what I mean? And they didn't seem to want to know us that way, either.

"We'd like to get together with them sometime . . . they were real nice. But I wonder if we'd ever get to really know each other? I mean, all we talked about was how we differed. That doesn't seem like much basis for a relationship. I wonder why that is, really? I think they know the Lord all right. I wonder why we couldn't relate to each other as Christians, instead of as Presbyterians and, well, whatever they were? It seems a shame."

13

CREATED AS ONE

People have always felt tensions, strains, distance in their relationships with others. Sometimes the distances have been great, marked with antagonism and hatred. And this is only natural. It's this way in every human society. People are people.

But according to the Bible it's different for one group of people. The Bible says that God has done something about the differences, the strains, the distance for Christ's people. For Christians, God has brought hostility to an end and has, in Christ, created unity where before there was only division (cf. Eph. 2:14-16).

For Christians, who have in common the Person of Jesus Christ and the reconciliation to God He worked on the cross, *unity can become a way of life.* And the tensions, like those in the four cases above, can be replaced by oneness.

For the Christian, the oneness which God established through His Son can be experienced in every relationship of life. Christians can become one in their homes, on their church boards, in their church fellowships—and, beyond their own churches, in their relationships with others who know Christ too, despite denominational lines, color or appearance, or other differences.

This unity, this oneness in the Spirit, is our right and our possession in Christ. And we can experience it as we reach out to appropriate the reality of what God has done in creating us *one.*

This is what this book is about. About becoming what God's Word says we are . . . one in the Spirit.

14

Deep down I believe each Christian feels the need to experience unity with others in Christ's body. I know I do. So, like you, I'm exploring in this book. Reaching out, trying to open myself up to others, searching in God's Word to find out how He makes it possible for me to live in oneness and unity with others.

And because I trust God's Word, as you do, I'm enthusiastic as I set out in this quest to understand and experience oneness in the Spirit. May God the Father, who planned oneness for us in eternity past, and God the Son, who paid the price of unity in His own blood, and God the Spirit, who makes us one, guide our thoughts and our lives as we reach out to become what we are.

QUEST 1

Bible passage to explore
Ephesians 2:11-22
What groups are contrasted here?
Why have they been antagonists?
What has Christ's cross meant for them?
What is their relationship to each other now?
What differences will the new relationship make
in the feelings of each? In the behavior?

2

No Longer Strangers

"My motives are right."

"It's not enough."

"But I only want what's best for you."

"It's not enough."

"Then, what *is* enough?"

Ever had a conversation like this? Or have you ever made plans, trying to do what's right, and have them all go wrong?

It's all too easy to try your best, to act out of the best motives . . . and be wrong. Good intentions are never enough.

That's what Jesus pointed out to His disciples when He warned them, "If your eye is defective your whole body is in the dark. If, then, the light within you grows dark—how dense a darkness!" (Matt. 6:22,23). When you think you see what isn't there or fail to see what is there, every subsequent action is affected.

An uncle of mine stepped outside his north woods cabin one night and, looking up, saw the eyes of a porcupine peering down at him from a tree. He hurried inside, got his shotgun, and fired up at the two points of light . . . and missed. He fired again. And again. Still the eyes seemed to peer down at him.

At last he realized that what he saw were two stars, showing through the branches.

Because his eyes had been mistaken, his whole body had taken actions—getting the gun, raising it, firing it—that were empty and useless.

He thought his actions made sense. He intended to kill an animal that had been gnawing on and killing some of his young trees. But his good intentions weren't enough. His eye had been defective.

It's like this in all of life. Our well-intentioned actions are never enough. They must be based on accurate perception. As Jesus warned, "If your eye is defective your whole body is in the dark."

More than once Jesus had to correct His disciples because they had distorted vision. Like the time He told the disciples about His approaching death, and Peter took Him aside to argue. Peter's motives were right. He didn't want his Lord to suffer the agonies of the cross. But Peter didn't see the whole picture. Peter didn't understand why Jesus had to die. And Jesus rebuked Peter: "Get away from Me, Satan, for you are not taking God's viewpoint, but men's" (Mark 8:33).

TAKING GOD'S VIEWPOINT

This is a hard thing for us to do, because we are human beings, with limited vision and with perceptions distorted by the clutter of man's way of looking at life. But it is vital that we do come to see life and its great issues from God's vewpoint.

17

We need to clear our eyes of distortions that we're often not even aware exist.

Clearing our eyes is particularly important when we approach a topic like "becoming one in the Spirit." Over the years we've developed our own, very human ways of seeing other people, ways that often are distortions of God's viewpoint. In thinking about relationships within Christ's Church, we need to understand how we've learned to look at each other. Then we need to evaluate our approach by God's.

Classification. One way we normally relate to others is to classify them. For instance, when a person is introduced to another, what kinds of things are said? "Charlie, I'd like you to meet Harry Brown, the dentist"/Or, "Charlie, I'd like you to meet Harry Brown. He runs the Mobil station in town"/Or, "Charlie, this is Mavis Brown. She teaches third grade."

Somehow, when we're introduced, it's not enough just to present the person. We have to classify him. We have to say what he does or state some other association. "He's an Elk."/"He's a member of our church."

Differences. A peculiar thing about the way we classify others is that we usually look for and try to state *differences.* As a high schooler I was deeply conscious of differences between myself and many of my schoolmates. They were *girls.* I was so conscious of the difference, and so painfully shy, that when I saw one of these different people, a girl, walking toward me on the street, I'd cross over so I wouldn't have to meet her!

18

Later I joined the Navy and quickly learned to classify people in other ways. In particular, there were Officers . . . and enlisted men. I had friends who were enlisted men. But Officers? Well, I always felt uncomfortable with them. They were *Up*, and I was *down*. I didn't feel free to even think about making friends with an Officer.

Barriers. That's what differences begin to be, barriers that block people away from each other as persons.

When I got out of the Navy, I went to seminary and met a guy there I liked very much . . . until I discovered he'd been a Navy Officer. Suddenly the liking I'd felt was overcome by that old feeling of *looking up*. And my classification of him, by his difference from me, became a barrier that blocked me from developing a relationship with him.

All of these factors: classifying, awareness of difference, and a sense of barrier, are basic to the ways that people see each other. It's very human, very natural . . . and tragically wrong for Christians.

BLOCKED OFF

There are several reasons why it's wrong to view other persons in these very natural perspectives. One reason is that when we meet another person, classify him, become aware of our differences, and erect our barriers, we build walls that God doesn't intend be there.

We even build walls within the church.

When I was first converted, I sensed a great difference between myself and non-Christians. That difference went far beyond the smoking and drinking issues my church stressed. That sense of difference was good. There *was* a difference . . . and is.

But soon I began to classify fellow Christians. I learned the signs that make some Christians "good" Christians, and others "poor" Christians. Soon I became aware of the differences between Baptist-type Christians (me) and non-Baptists. Between Calvinist Christians (me) and Arminian Christians. Between non-denominational Christians (me) and denominational Christians. And before long, I only felt comfortable with "good," Baptist-type, Calvinistic, nondenominational Christians. I was ill at ease with all others!

My primary way of trying to relate to other Christians was to find out their differences from me, define and classify them by those differences, and then treat them accordingly. This way of living with people erected barriers and blocked me from knowing them. I found that once I had classified someone as "different," I didn't have any desire to know him or listen to him as a person. I was boxed away from a personal relationship with the people I met and worked with because of the way I identified them.

And that identity? "Different."

Not Baptistic.

Not Calvinistic.

Not nondenominational.

Not like me.

NO LONGER STRANGERS

If there were ever two groups of people who were *different* from each other, it was the Jews and Gentiles of New Testament days.

The Jews had a clear classification for the Gentiles. The Gentiles were Goyim, dogs. The barrier between them was so great that a good Jew would not even eat with a Gentile or enter his home. Between the two groups there had developed a consistent, rasping hostility.

And then something happened.

Jesus died on a cross for Jew and Gentile alike, and the Holy Spirit touched a band of Jesus' disciples. On the day of Pentecost, He fused them into the Church, a group of men and women who found a new relationship with each other in their common relationship to Jesus Christ.

The good news of forgiveness and new life in Jesus the Messiah spread through Jerusalem and Judea. More and more men and women were drawn into this strange companionship of Christ's Church. And the New Testament documents the closeness of their fellowship and love.

But then a jolting thing happened. God reached out and drew *Gentiles* to Jesus! These hated and rejected men, all the more hated because they represented an empire that kept the Jewish nation in subjection, responded to the love of Israel's crucified King. Jew and Gentile were suddenly fused into one body, one companionship of the cross.

As the Apostle Paul wrote to the Gentile church at Ephesus: "Now, through the blood of Christ,

21

you who were once outside the pale are with us inside the circle of God's love in Christ Jesus. For Christ is our living peace. He has made a unity of the conflicting elements of Jew and Gentile by breaking down the barrier which lay between us. By His sacrifice He removed the hostility of the law, with all its commandments and rules, and made in Himself out of the two, Jew and Gentile, one new man, thus producing peace. For He reconciled both to God by the sacrifice of one body on the cross, and by this act made utterly irrelevant the antagonism between them" (Eph. 2:13-16 PH).

The differences by which these men had classified each other suddenly didn't matter. The antagonism which had existed was made "utterly irrelevant."

Only one thing was relevant now. *Both, by the sacrifice of Christ on the cross, had been reconciled to God.*

The old identity of "Jew" and "Gentile" had been swallowed up in a new identity: *Christian.* And only this identity counted. How utterly at odds was this divine perspective with all their past conceptions of each other! And now Jew and Gentile alike were told to learn to live by God's viewpoint ... not their own.

It is to be the same with us today. The differences by which we classify fellow believers and the barriers we erect are to be broken down by the realization that in His cross Christ has reconciled both us and our brothers to God. If another person knows Christ, I need to see him as "inside the circle of God's love in Jesus" with me.

IDENTITY

It's hard for me to see every other Christian as within my own circle because I've been conditioned over many years to look at people from a human viewpoint. But as I look into the Bible, I discover that God has made His perspective clear.

How does God see us?

"Through your faith in Christ Jesus," the Bible says, "you are all sons of God" (Gal. 3:26). And John adds, "See what a wealth of love the Father has lavished on us, that we should be called the children of God. And we are. For this reason the world does not know us, because it did not know Him. Beloved ones, we are God's children now, and what we shall be has not yet been shown; but we know that when He appears we shall resemble Him, for we shall see Him as He is" (1 John 3:1-3).

The Bible makes it clear that all of us in our unredeemed state are dead to God. We are His creatures, yes, but not His spiritual children. Yet in Jesus Christ, God acted to give lost humanity life and hope. "God is rich in mercy," the Scriptures say. "He made us who were dead in trespasses, alive with Christ" (Eph. 2:4, 5). When God gave us life, it was His life, His heredity. People who had been disobedient and enemies of God were changed, were supernaturally reborn as His sons.

And this is our essential identity as Christians. Not "of such-and-such a church." Not "of this-or-that theology." But *God's sons, God's children.*

The Bible says the same thing in a very exciting,

slightly different way. It says we are the "brothers of Christ." The Book of Hebrews speaks of Christ tasting death for us and "bringing many sons to glory." And the writer goes on, "For the One who makes holy and those who are being made holy all have one Father, for which reason He is not ashamed to call them brothers, when He says, 'I shall proclaim Thy name to My brothers; in the midst of the congregation I shall sing Thy praise'" (Heb. 2:11, 12).

Now we share the life of God. Christ the Saviour looks at us and calls us "brother." And this is only right. For God has appointed us "to share the likeness of His Son, so that He might be the Firstborn among many brothers" (Rom. 8:29).

So this is what we are, children of God, and brothers of Jesus Christ. This is our supreme identity, and our identifying mark.

It's sometimes easy for us to wish we were important or well known. We wish we could do big things for God, as a famous evangelist or dedicated missionary. But any such identity: "Frank Brown, the famous evangelist," pales to insignificance beside the actual identity we bear: "Frank Brown ... God's child, Frank Brown ... Christ's brother." Nothing we might do could add any glory to this.

Somehow each of us as a Christian needs to grasp the glory of who he is in Christ. Each of us needs to begin to think of himself first of all, and most important of all, as God's child.

And then we need to look around us at our fellow Christians and realize who they are! If Jesus calls me brother and He also calls my fellow believer *brother*, how can I give him any other name? If God accepts him as His child, how can I exclude him and label him "different?"

I've been going to a church where, two years ago, a bearded young man began to attend. He was neat and clean. But that beard! He didn't *look* like the rest of us. And so some in the church turned away when he came near. One man in particular was openly critical and hostile, but never to the bearded one directly. He finally found out that the younger man had gone to the Bible school he himself had attended! Then he finally made the effort to speak to him.

It's easy to look at something like a beard and say, "He's different." It's easy to put up the barriers that block others out of our lives. But the beard was not his identity. His identity was: *our brother*.

This then helps me begin to see how I have to view other people in order to experience the oneness the Bible describes. Only one thing is basic. *Does another person have a personal relationship with Jesus Christ?* If he does, I need to see him as my brother. I cannot cut myself off from someone that my Father accepts as His child.

So the human way of viewing people—classifying them, seeking to define their differences from us, and then making barriers out of the differences—is ruled out for us Christians. Instead we have to clear our eyes of such distortions and learn to see each other from God's perspective. We need to learn to accept each other as members of a common family, as children of one Father.

25

QUEST 1

Bible passage to explore
Acts 11:1-18

Why were the Jewish Christians upset with Peter?

What did Peter learn through the vision?

What need was there for the sign given (vv. 15-17)?

What was the response to Peter's report? (v. 18)

What principles presented in this chapter are illustrated in this Bible incident?

QUEST 2

Personal applications
Identity

Think of three people, one you know well, one you do not know yet, and one who strikes you as "different" from you. Record briefly your feelings about each and how these feelings affect your relationship with each.

Now try to think of each from God's viewpoint. What difference does this make in your attitude toward each?

3

One Body

Christian and Missionary Alliance missionary Adriaan van der Bijl reports the impact of the Gospel on tribal groups in West Irian, Indonesia. When revival came, so did reconciliation for men who only a few months earlier had been at war, killing and even eating each other.

World Vision magazine reported, "After a recent baptismal service, the two estranged groups lined up opposite each other as one leader shouted, 'We have always been your enemies. Shall we continue to fight?' The answer came, 'We want to be one with our brothers.' The two groups rushed toward each other to embrace in demonstration of new-found Christian love."*

Something happens when Christians grasp the reality of their identity in Jesus Christ. When we come to the amazing realization that we are truly God's children, when we begin to look at fellow believers as brothers and sisters, then we "want to be one with our brothers."

---

*"*Globe at a Glance*," World Vision, *May 1972, p. 3.*

THE DESIRE TO BE ONE

The desire to be one with our brothers is a reflection of God's desire for us. Christ expressed God's concern in what is known as His "high priestly" prayer, recorded in John 17. Here, praying for all believers, He reveals God's yearning for His children, "I am . . . praying . . . for those who will believe in Me through their message, so that all may be one, as Thou, Father, art in Me, and I in Thee, so they may be in Us, and so that the world may believe that Thou hast sent Me. I have given them the glory which Thou hast given to Me, so that they may be one as We are one, I in them and Thou in Me, so that they may be completed into one, that the world may recognize that Thou hast sent Me and hast loved them as Thou hast loved Me" (John 17:20-32).

Christ's prayer, repeated three times, that believers might have a unique unity expressed here as "being one," was offered just before His crucifixion. What an appropriate time! A few short hours later, Jesus Christ went to the cross to accomplish in His death exactly what He had asked. The Bible says that He died that He might create of antagonistic groups and hostile individuals "one new person." Jesus gave Himself to unite into one those who had been separated (cf. Eph. 2:13-16).

It's striking to realize that God so wants us to be one in the Spirit that Christ willingly endured the cross. Yes, certainly His death was for individuals, for the remission of sins and for forgiveness. But Christ's death had an impact beyond the provision of new life for believing men and women. *Christ's death brought individuals together in a new relationship, forming us into one.*

Because the Cross and the Resurrection were effective in accomplishing God's purposes, the Bible speaks of oneness as a reality. The Bible says we *are* one body. "There is neither Jew nor Greek, there is neither slave nor freeman, there is neither male nor female, because you are all one in Christ Jesus" (Gal. 3:28). And again, "The many of us form one body in Christ" (Rom. 12:5).

So when revival came to the two pagan tribes in West Irian, and they rushed out to love those whom they had hated and tried to kill, they were responding to a reality. They had been enemies. But now in Christ they were one. God the Holy Spirit had cleared their eyes and changed their hearts, and they were eager to experience *all* that Christ had died to bring them.

DISTORTIONS

It's amazing to me to see these Stone Age-like people, so new to Christian faith, eagerly responding to the message of oneness. It's amazing when we realize that you and I, in our civilized world, knowing Christ so long, have often failed to respond as they!

But then, there was hesitancy in the Early Church too. Men who were Christians, brothers and sisters in Christ, joined together in one body, could fail to experience oneness in the Spirit. The Bible speaks of unity and harmony in some churches. In others the New Testament writers describe "strife, jealousy, ugly temper, sectarianism, slander, gossiping, conceit, disharmony" (2 Cor. 12:20).

We *are* one. But we do not automatically experience the oneness! We *are* one. But we don't all cry, "We want to be one with our brothers!"

DISTORTED VIEWS

Failure to experience our oneness may go back to something mentioned in the last chapter. Our vision is clouded. Our perception of unity may be wrong. We've tended to look at unity and oneness from a human point of view and failed to realize that God's perspective is different.

So it's helpful to think a bit about the way men seek unity.

We look for what we have in common. This is the first, often unconscious step in seeking to establish a unity. We see it in the excited report of a teen-age girl: "Mom, did you know Jack likes art too? We both like to oil paint, and he likes landscapes best, just like me! And you know what? We both like peanut butter and banana sandwiches! Isn't that just wild?"

Somehow we see the little things we have in common as strands to link us with others.

This is true in most relationships. Labor unions were formed by men who had their work in common and felt a need to join forces to work toward common goals. Political parties are formed, initially, around some common core of concern, as the Republican party was born of very diverse elements because of a common desire to stop the ex-

30

pansion of slavery into new territories. Friendships also take shape around things held in common: a common job, common interests, common likes and dislikes.

So we tend to reach out to other people to find things we like or do or believe in common. And we use these little links to draw us closer to each other.

We look for differences from others. Usually the little links of common likes and dislikes aren't enough to build in-depth relationships. They may be enough for acquaintance but not enough for unity. So when people feel a need to band together, they tend to stress their differences from others "outside" their group. For instance, it wasn't enough that men have work in common to create unions. The union movement grew because working men also had a common enemy . . . the great management combines that they felt exploited them. And so the workers were unified *against* an enemy.

It is the same with political parties. Every four years, before the presidential nominating conventions, there is a great deal of competition and contention. Supporters of one candidate all but castigate opposing candidates. Bitter fights sometimes arise over platform issues.

Then the nominating convention is over. And the party is struggling to regain an overall unity. How will they do it? Not only by stressing what they have in common ("We're all Democrats, after all"), but also by stressing differences shared against the "enemy." ("Our task this fall is to beat the Republicans!")

It takes things like this to hold people together. Men don't by nature love each other or submerge their selfish desires for the sake of unity. What is held in common isn't enough for unity. There needs to be some great defining difference from others . . . who ideally can be viewed as "enemy" . . . to hold people together.

But even this isn't really enough for men anxious to build unity.

We push for conformity. Associations of people are always unstable. There's always the danger of betrayal of the group. People recognize (even if some won't admit) that sin is a reality. Because people are warped by sin, they are not really trustworthy.

When there is a desire for unity, there are usually accompanying fears and suspicions. The usual result is some demand within the group for conformity.

An uncle of mine worked in Detroit during years of union strife. He was a shop steward, representing the working men and presenting their demands and needs to management. In one particular case, my uncle met for several hours with his plant managers, and, convinced that they were right in rejecting a particular worker demand, agreed with them and took a stand against his fellows. That night as he left the plant he was beaten by a number of the men. They were convinced he had sold them out, and probably only the fact that his wife was an invalid prevented them from crippling him!

This is a vivid example of the demand for conformity. *If you are going to be with us, you must in everything think and feel and act as we do!* If you are going to identify yourself with us and against them, *you must be like us!*

Examples of this phenomenon exist all around us. The other day I was in a store and saw a "typical hippie." He wore a ragged beard and long hair, a red headband, dirty jeans and very little shirt. And I thought, *How many have I seen that look just like him?* His "difference" was so totally the same as the "difference" of others. He rebelled against the system . . . and accepted a conformity even more restrictive.

I could give an example from the other side. I visited a lawyer two weeks ago. His hair was neatly cut. He wore a tie and a conservative shirt and suit. He carried a briefcase. And he sat in a paneled office. He looked just the same as the others with offices in his building. To belong, he too conformed.

In all this we see a notion that is a most natural and almost universal human viewpoint. If we have things in common, if we see ourselves as different from some others, and if we get rid of differences within our group (conformity) . . . we'll have unity. To unify . . . to be together . . . *we have to be alike!*

And so unity comes to be confused with, and equated to, conformity!

With this in mind we're struck by a strange thing when we look into the Bible and see what God says about unity. For in the Bible we discover that God does not create unity by removing differences.

No, God *makes unity out of the differences!*

The Phillips version puts this truth very neatly in Ephesians 2. "He [God] has made a unity of the conflicting elements." And, again, by the cross Christ "made utterly irrelevant the antagonism" between differing groups and individuals.

The primary reference, of course, is to Jew and Gentile. These two groups had totally different life-styles. They had different ways of dressing and acting, different traditions, different attitudes about many things. The differences between these two groups were far greater, for instance, than the differences between older and younger generations we hear so much of these days. Yet in Jesus Christ, God put these two conflicting elements together and made unity.

God didn't demand that either change. The Gentile didn't have to become a Jew. Or the Jew begin to think and feel like a Gentile. Each kept his own individuality. It was of diverse elements that God made His unity, His one body. God's way of making people one was not the way of conformity.

Not everyone in the early days of the Church understood this. As the young Church struggled to integrate Gentile converts into what had been an

34

exclusively Jewish faith, some began to insist on conformity as the price of acceptance. "Some men came down from Judea [to the Gentile church at Antioch] and began to teach the brothers, saying, 'Unless you are circumcised according to the custom of Moses you cannot be saved'" (Acts 15:1, PH). These men felt intensely that to be a Christian a person must also become a Jew.

The Early Church met to consider this utterly basic question about the nature of the fellowship God's Spirit was forming.

The result? The Church rejected the pressures of those who insisted on conformity as the price of unity and responded, "Surely the fact is that it is by the grace of the Lord Jesus that we are saved by faith, just as they are!" (Acts 15:9, PH).

The response went to the root of the issue. *The fact is . . .* both alike are saved by faith and are recipients of God's grace. *The fact is . . .* God has accepted Jews and Gentiles as His children. Other superficial differences did not matter! As Paul would later write, "God has made utterly irrelevant" any antagonism based on past differences.

Such differences simply do not count when the reality of relationship with God and each other is recognized.

This discovery of the Early Church is all too easy for us to forget. *God does not insist that a person surrender his individuality in inconsequential things.* God does not insist that we conform to each other as the price of unity. Instead, God insists that we recognize other Christians as brothers and reject pressuring them to conform.

And this is hard. In almost every church there are people who differ. I know churches in which some people are urging "renewal"—pushing for changes in traditional structures, talking of new life and experiences for believers. Others in the same churches are afraid, concerned that the changes urged mean the loss of something that is important and a part of their Christian heritage. It's easy for people in each group to become upset with the other, to focus on their differences, and to put on pressure to make others conform to their way of thinking, their way of expressing their faith in Jesus.

It's so easy to be human.

But this is not God's way of making unity. God does not insist that every Christian think and feel and act like every other. God does not insist that every Christian *conform*. Instead, God takes the differences and purposely puts them together to make one new man.

DIFFERENCES COUNT

In one sense, differences between people don't count in the Church . . . we are to reject conformity as a way of working toward unity. At the same time, the Bible say differences *do* count in the sense that God has a purpose in making us different.

Why does God purposely fit together people who are different to make His unity? I think we can see why a cook uses different ingredients to prepare a dish. My wife makes a fine tuna casserole. She uses rice, tuna, mushroom soup, and green peas. She cooks them carefully, making sure the peas remain firm. Then she blends them together to make one delicious dish.

Nothing in the casserole has lost its identity. I can still distinguish the pieces of mushroom. The peas retain their character and shape and color. The elements don't conform . . . they *blend*. And in blending together they create a flavorful meal that none could match if kept apart and served alone.

It's something like this with the Church. When believers are blending together, each retaining his individuality and outlook, something better results than if we isolate ourselves and associate only with those who are just like us.

Several passages in the Bible speak of the importance of differences within Christ's body. In Romans and I Corinthians people are pictured as members of a human body—as feet, or hands, or eyes, or mouths. And each Christian is said to be able, because of his different gifts and abilities, to contribute something distinct to the whole. "For just as the body is one and has many members, while all the numerous parts of the body compose one body, so it is with Christ" (1 Cor. 12:12). And Paul goes on to say that all—Jews, Greeks, slaves, and free men (and who can imagine more distinctly different life-styles and ideas than between these groups!)—have been united by the Holy Spirit into one body (1 Cor. 12:13).

And, the argument continues, *these differences are essential to health!* "The fact is there are many parts, but only one body. So that the eye cannot say to the hand, 'I don't need you!' nor, again, can the head say to the feet, 'I don't need you!' On the contrary . . . God has harmonized the whole body . . . that the body should work together as a whole with all the members in sympathetic relationship with one another" (1 Cor. 12:20-25, PH).

How clearly, then, the Bible's teaching on spiritual gifts illustrates how God *values* the differences between the people in His body! His way of making unity, of making us one, is to use the differences . . . *not* to suppress them through conformity.

A NEW PERSPECTIVE

The Bible, then, gives us a new perspective on unity. The natural man's way of seeking unity is to (1) look for little things he has in common with others, then (2) find differences between his group and others, and finally (3) increasingly insist that those who are *with* him be *like* him.

God's way is different. God asserts that (1) we *are* a unity because we have Jesus in common, (2) our differences are irrelevant in this "one body" relationship, and finally (3) our differences are intended by God to blend together, enriching all of us in our oneness.

For this divine kind of unity, many of our old attitudes and ideas about people are irrelevant . . . and wrong.

QUEST 1

Bible passage to explore
Ephesians 4:1-16

38

What important things do believers have in common?

In what ways do we differ?

What is the purpose of differences in the body of Christ?

What is the result of a "blended" body, functioning and unified?

4

Distinguishing Things That Differ

God did something totally new when He formed Christ's Church. He made unity out of differences. Going against the grain of human nature that insists on conformity, God put into one body people who are different but who share one central, essential bond. Members of Christ's Church have God's life within, won on Calvary, received by us through simple faith.

But we're still human. It's a jolt for us to change the pattern of our thinking and feeling about other people. It's hard to see each other from God's perspective alone. So the differences that exist still bother us. We still try to live together as men of the world do, associating because we're like each other, pushing others away who don't conform to our practices and distinctives.

The Early Church experienced this same thing. "I heard," Paul wrote to the Corinthians, "that as you meet as a congregation there are divisions among you." And he notes, "I do not commend you" (cf 1 Cor. 11:17-19). Differences are not in themselves wrong. In fact, talking about our differences can lead to better understanding of God's Word and will. But when the differences lead to conflict, to judging others, to party spirit, then they break the unity of the body. And when this happens, "You are still unspiritual. Insofar as you entertain jealousy and contentiousness, are you not unspiritual and do you not behave like the unconverted?" (1 Cor. 3:3, 4)

Thus, the Bible says, "Avoid foolish controversies, genealogies, strife, and wranglings about the law, for they are futile and purposeless. Have nothing to do with a factious person after a first and second warning, aware that such a person is perverted and goes on sinning, and is self-condemned" (Titus 3:1-11).

As Christ once warned, "Any kingdom that is divided against itself goes to ruin, and any city or house that is divided against itself cannot stand" (Matt. 12:25). How tragic when we permit differences to dominate in our relationships with other Christians and to divide the very body of Christ!

DIFFERENCES THAT DIVIDE

The Bible deals specifically with a variety of differences that may—but should not—divide the body of Christ.* Many of these differences are hard for us to accept as irrelevant. Though the Bible says we are to ignore them, they are sometimes very important to us. In looking at them, we must remember to subject ourselves to the Word of God; we must be willing to reexamine our practices and our beliefs in the light of God's Word.

Social differences. James graphically sketches the divisive impact of social differences in the Early Church (cf. James 2:1-9). He tells of two men who come to church. One is rich, well dressed, looked up to in the community. The other is poor and shabbily clad. What happens? The rich man is enthusiastically welcomed and ushered to a front seat. The poor man is pushed off to a back seat in the overflow room.

What does the Bible say about this kind of thing? It says, "Have you not discriminated among your own and become judges with evil thoughts?" (2:4) Christ's law is to love your neighbor (2:8). "If you show partiality, then you are practicing sin" (2:9).

There are all sorts of ways we show partiality in our fellowships today. Do we welcome the black (white) man? In *just the same way* that we welcome the most respected white (black) in our community? How about the bearded youth? Are we as glad to have him join us Sunday morning as we are to have the couple with three small children to swell our Sunday School? How do we respond to

Chapter 7 deals with sin, a difference which is to divide.

41

rich and poor? Does education or business success lead us to welcome some and reject or be lukewarm to others?

According to God's Word, when we discriminate and judge people by such outward things, we sin. God's love for the brethren knows no such distinctions. And as we reach out in love to others who may be different we'll experience the rich reward that comes when the body of Christ is at one.

Practices. Some of the hardest things for us to accept as inconsequential are those that we have chosen to mark off believers from unbelievers, or spiritual from unspiritual. I mean the kind of thing we think of when someone says, "A Christian doesn't. . . ." Or, "A Christian should. . . ."

In my early life as a believer I was in a church with well-defined lists of "shoulds" and "shouldn'ts." I recall clearly a member of our church trying to hide a cigarette behind his hand when the pastor and I approached. I remember my deep distrust of a minister from another church whom I found smoking a pipe and my horror at learning a navy chaplain had actually drunk wine with a meal in England, where apparently some Christians do it regularly! Somehow these things —even the "shoulds"—became barriers that cut me off from brothers and sisters in Christ.

Was I wrong?

The Pharisees (who had extensive lists too) were rebuked by Jesus one day. These devout men had observed Jesus' disciples eating lunch without (ritually) washing their hands. So they asked, "Why do your disciples behave contrary to the elders' traditions?" Jesus shocked them with a stinging attack that you can read in Mark 7:5-13. His main point was clearly stated: "Vainly they worship Me, when teaching human regulations as doctrines. You let go of God's commandments to cling to human tradition" (7:7, 8).

This is a point we ought to seriously consider. Jesus said, "Just as I have loved you, so you should love one another" (John 13:34). And this He called His new command. When you or I draw back from a brother because of what is human regulation (for the Bible does *not* say, "Do not smoke," or even, "Do not drink any alcoholic beverages"), then how do we differ from the Pharisee? We have let go of God's specific command, giving higher priority to a human regulation (no matter how reasonable and right the regulation may be).

Well, how then do we handle such differences? (And I speak as a nonsmoker and nondrinker from conviction, just as you probably are.) First, we remember that the heart of Christian faith is not found in our practices. Jesus went on to say, as recorded in the Mark passage, "Do you not perceive that whatever enters from the outside cannot defile a person? . . . What comes out of the man defiles him, for from within, out of a man's heart wicked thoughts emerge" (Mark 7:18-21). What counts with God, and what must count with us, is a man's heart for God, his motives, and character. We have no right to condemn or judge him on the externals.

Second, we accept the fact that such practices are not always an accurate indicator of relationship with God. Paul, writing to the Colossians, says about them: "Don't touch this! Don't taste that! Don't handle the other! All these are destined to wear out; they are governed by human injunctions and instructions, such as have, to be sure, a suggestion of wisdom by self-imposed worship and humiliation and unsparing severity of the body, but are of no value in combating fleshly indulgence" (Col. 2:21-23). Lists of proscribed and prescribed practices may look good and spiritual, but actually be expressions of self-righteousness. They are not infallible indicators of our growth as Christians.

Third, we *welcome* as a brother one whose practices differ from ours. Speaking of a case in which the difference was one of conviction about diet, the Bible says, "The one who eats should not feel contempt for him who abstains, nor should the one who abstains censure him who eats, *for God has* accepted him" (Rom. 14:3). And again we face the basic issue. If my heavenly Father owns another person as His child, how can I reject him? He *is* my brother, and I am to welcome and love him for who he is . . . not for what he does.

So the human way of dealing with differences is again rejected by God. We cannot insist on conformity as the price of acceptance. We cannot demand that others *be like us* before we welcome them in Christian love. We have no right to feel contempt or to censure. If a man or woman knows Christ as personal Saviour, God has accepted him. And so must you and I.

Doctrinal differences. In 1 Corinthians Paul deals with another divisive issue. This is a clear case of disagreement on doctrinal grounds, not a basic doctrine like salvation by faith or the trustworthiness of God's Word, but doctrine nevertheless. It seems that some in the church visited temple meat markets on their daily shopping trips. These markets were open behind the temples of pagan gods and goddesses and were stocked with the meat of animals offered to the temple idol. Because worshipers brought only the best animals, the best meat was sold there.

Such shopping scandalized other believers. This was trafficking with idols! Christ had delivered believers from Satan's kingdom. How could Christians have anything to do with pagan worship or support it through their purchases?

The Christians who visited the temple meat markets, however, did so with a clear conscience. They knew that idols had no real existence. They were convinced that the superstitions of the idol worshipers were just this—empty superstitions. And so, thankful that they knew the true and living God, and perhaps a bit smug about their superior knowledge of the real nature of idolatry, they enjoyed the meat as God's provision and gift.

How does the Bible handle such conflict over doctrine? We read, "It is easy to think that we 'know' over problems like this. But we should remember that while knowledge may make a man look big, it is only love that can make him grow to his full stature. For whatever a man may know, he still has a lot to learn; but if he loves God, he is opening his whole life to the spirit of God" (1 Cor. 8:1-3, PH). *The Bible says that we are to deal even*

45

*with doctrinal differences more on the basis of love
than of "knowledge."*

This is terribly hard to accept. Because here we
know there is a right answer. There *is* revealed
truth . . . God has given us His Word, and we can
know what is right. Then why aren't we simply
told to insist that all accept the truths revealed
there? Why aren't we told to separate from those
who do not accept what God's Word presents as
the right answer?

The reason is given in the verses already quoted.
"Only love can make a man grow to his full stature." And, "If he loves God, he is opening his
whole life to the Spirit of God." We must remember that people can change their doctrinal
views, and that an atmosphere of love is conducive
to truth.

Look at it this way. Suppose you and I begin to
talk about eternal security, and soon it is clear we
differ. In fact, we take opposite sides. So each of us
determines to correct the other, to show him that
he is wrong.

What happens to each of us? First of all, the
issue has become very personal. For me to change
my position now means more than accepting biblical evidence. It means I have to admit you've *won*,
and I've *lost*. Down inside that's hard for me . . . or
for you! So rather than give in, we each work
harder to prove our point. Soon we're not listening
to each other, or to the passages of Scripture each
cites. Trying to win, we think only of finding Bible
passages that seem to support our own position.
We are not submitting ourselves to God's Word;

46

*we are trying to use God's Word to support our
ideas.* We have closed our hearts to God.

What a different approach Scripture suggests!
Yes, there is a right answer. There is objective
truth. But we don't know it automatically; we
"still have a lot to learn." So the first issue when
we find a point of doctrinal difference is not *"who
is right,"* but *what will help us learn what is right?*

And God's answer to this is, *love.*

"If he loves God, he is opening his whole life to
the Spirit of God." And remember, the Spirit is the
Teacher who "will guide you into all truth" (John
16:13). Our ministry to each other when we differ
doctrinally is to help each other love God more,
trusting the Holy Spirit to work in a life that is
opened to Him.

How different this is from the bitterness and
anger that sometimes grow when we differ on doctrine! How different from the attacking and striking out at one another! And how right!

When a man named Apollos came to Ephesus, he
began to preach about Jesus, though he had at the
time only heard the preaching of John the Baptist.
He wasn't aware of the events of the Crucifixion
and Resurrection or of the Holy Spirit's coming. The
Bible says, "He began to speak freely in the synagogue." And then comes the exciting insight into
the gentleness and love of Christian brothers. "But
Priscilla and Aquila, after listening to him, took
him aside and explained the way of God more accurately to him" (Acts 18:26). They listened to
him. They didn't jump up in the synagogue to correct and argue with him. They listened to him. Af-

terward they took him aside, where there would be no embarrassment, and explained the way of God more accurately to him.

How much we need this attitude in the church today. Sensitive, gentle love, that listens, and takes people aside to share the way of God more accurately. Under love, Apollos' life was opened to God, and he became a leader in the Church of Christ.

FREEDOM TO DIFFER

The Bible teaches us, then, that we must give others the freedom to differ. And we must accept one another as brothers in spite of differences which might grate on our personalities, or differences which in the world would be just cause for separation. God says, "Welcome the weak believer, and do not criticize his views" (Rom. 14:1). Welcome him as a brother, to help him love God and open up his life to God.

But then we wonder. Won't this destroy the purity of the Church? Won't unbelievers sneak in? Won't heresy take root? Don't we have to stand fast and contend for the faith?

Yes, we stand and contend . . . with those *outside* the Body. We accept, and love, and welcome our brothers.

Then how does the church remain pure? It doesn't remain totally pure. Jesus told His disciples not to try uprooting counterfeit believers. They were likely to injure true believers in the process (Matt. 13:24-30; 36-43). The Son of man Himself will separate them, at the end of the age.

But even now the separation process is taking

place. The Bible tells of men who went out from the fellowship of the Early Church, separating *themselves*. Why? "They went out from us but they never belonged to us; for had they been ours, they would have remained with us" (1 John 2:19).

God has another way of removing important differences: by the teaching of sound doctrine. Paul reminds Timothy of this responsibility (for we are to hold to the Word of God as His own inspired and trustworthy truth). But note the attitude in which we teach truth. "The Lord's servant must not be a man of strife; he must be kind to all, ready and able to teach: he must have patience and the ability to gently correct those who oppose his message. He must always bear in mind the possibility that God will give them a different outlook, and that they may come to know the truth" (2 Tim. 2:24, 25).

How good to be free to accept our brothers who differ, just because they are our brothers! How good to know that while we all have a lot to learn, we have a God who is eager to teach us! And that loving each other, and helping each other love God, opens up all of our lives to His Spirit!

QUEST 1

Bible passages to study
Matthew 9:9-13
What differences did objectors complain of?
How did Jesus answer them?
What does this teach us?
Compare also Luke 19:1-10; Mark 2:14-17.
James 3:13-18

What principles developed in this chapter are restated in this passage?

Can "jealousy and rivalry" ever be sourced in spiritual concern?

How can characteristics of the "wisdom from above" be applied in dealing with the kinds of differences discussed in this chapter?

5

Follow the Way of Love

It kept cropping up in the last chapter. What's more important than social differences? The "royal law [royal, for it was proclaimed by King Jesus], love your neighbor" (James 2:8). What cuts across our differences in practices and conviction? Love. What principle guides us in dealing with doctrinal disputes? Love.

No wonder we read, "Make love your greatest quest" (1 Cor. 14:1). No wonder there is a constant emphasis throughout the New Testament on love as the distinguishing mark of Christ's Church.

"Above all else," writes Peter, "cherish intense love for one another" (1 Peter 4:8).

Paul mentions love over and over. "Let all that you do be done in love" (1 Cor. 16:14). "Bear patiently with one another in a loving way, making every effort to preserve the unity of the Spirit in the bond of peace" (Eph 4:2, 3). "It is not necessary to write you about brotherly love, for you yourselves are taught by God to love one another, and you are practicing it toward all the brothers throughout Macedonia. But we appeal to you, brothers, to keep advancing in it . . ." (1 Thes. 4:9-11).

Three times John records the repeated words of Jesus Christ, "I give you a new command, 'Love one another.' Just as I have loved you, so you should love one another. By this everyone will recognize that you are My disciples, if you love one another" (John 13:34, 35; cf. 15:12, 17).

Love, then, has the highest priority in the Church, which is Christ's body. And learning to love our brothers in Christ is the key to oneness in the Spirit. Without love there can be no unity. With love, differences can be submerged, and we can move, in one body, to spiritual growth and outreach.

LOVE'S IMPACT

Alan couldn't understand love. He'd been brought up on a farm in upper New York state, and had known only toil from earliest memory. His father was a dour man, who drove himself and his family and never gave a word of praise. Like any child, Alan desperately needed his father's approval and tried hard to please him. But Alan's father never seemed to approve. He'd look over a completed job, and his only words would be criticism of any imperfection.

When Alan got into high school, he went out for wrestling. Though small, he was quick and strong and began to win consistently. And he was ranked statewide. Alan's father never had time for his matches but did attend the state tourney. And Alan won! That night, on the way home, Al's dad had only one thing to say: "You let your opponents get too many points."

When I knew Alan he was an unhappy person. He struggled to do his best but was burdened by fear of failure. He struggled to reach perfection but could not be satisfied with his best efforts. Alan had no joy in his work; every day was tinged with the misery of trying over and over to prove himself.

Many of us have known the kind of "love" that Alan knew, and our personalities share his scars. We doubt our own worth. We act out of fear, constantly trying to win the approval of others by what we do. We demand perfection in ourselves and can never believe that others accept and appreciate us.

How desperately we need to know God's kind of love, love that "casts out" such fears (1 John 4:18)! For Jesus' love is *totally unlike* the love Alan, and so many of us, have experienced. Jesus' love asserts, "You are important. You're worthy, not for what you do, but for what you are." Certainly the Bible is blunt in its assertion that we are sinners. We haven't lived up to God's standards. "All have sinned, and fall short of God's moral excellence" (Rom. 3:23). We have not and cannot earn God's approval. It was not for works of righteousness which we have done that Jesus reached out to save us.

Some look at this portrait of sin and flail the human race as worthless. We do read in God's revelation that our common sin incurs both guilt and shame. But this is not the whole picture. Man is sinner, *but even as sinner he is of value to God!*

The Bible speaks of "Christ's dying for us when we were still sinners" (Rom. 5:8). Thus He showed us His love. The Bible's portrait of our sin and helplessness only serves to reinforce the amazing truth that persons are important. How important? Well, to God we were worth the inexpressible cost of His Son's lifeblood spilled on Calvary's cross. "Love is manifested in this," the Bible says, "not that we loved God, but that He loved us and sent His Son as an atoning sacrifice for our sins" (1 John 4:10).

This unconditional, worth-asserting love is a different kind of love from that Alan knew. This is a freeing love. Knowing this love, we do not have to fear, because we know our acceptance is not based on our efforts. We don't have to prove ourselves over and over. We are of worth as persons. Duty and struggle are replaced by the joy for returning the love of Him who loves us. With our motivation changed, with the focus shifted from us and our efforts to God and His love, we grow and change.

Alan's idea of love was shaped by what he experienced in his relationship with his father. His personality is a reflection of the kind of love he was given. Each of us has been so shaped. And each of us can be freed to grow and change by experiencing

53

God's kind of love in the fellowship of Christ's Church. "Love one another" is the most repeated command in the New Testament. And no wonder. Love opens our lives to God.

"JUST AS" LOVE

The Bible shows us how to love each other. Jesus said, "*Just as* I have loved you, so you should love one another" (John 13:34). So we look to Jesus Christ and see love expressed. Then we love "just as" He.

One Bible passage draws together seven significant features of Jesus' love. And these features are enclosed between two statements of the command we're considering! "This is My command, that you love one another as I have loved you. No one has greater love than this; to lay down his life for his friends. You are my friends if you do what I command you. I no longer call you slaves, for a slave does not know what his master is doing, but I have called you friends because I have acquainted you with everything I heard from My Father. You have not chosen Me, but I have chosen you and appointed you to go out and produce fruit and that your fruit should be permanent, so that whatever you ask the Father in My name He may grant you. This is My command to you: 'Love one another'" (John 15:12-17).

(1) *Laying down our lives* (v. 12). This is the first feature of "just as" love. Jesus' love led Him to the cross. He literally gave His life for us, that we might come to God (cf. Rom. 5:6-11). In His days on earth, Jesus gave His life for others, too.

Jesus was often tired, but He moved on to preach to those in the next town. Jesus was hungry, but He thought first of the crowds that followed Him and gave them bread. Jesus was busy, but He stopped when a blind beggar called out to Him. He turned and spoke to a chronically ill woman who touched Him as He passed. Jesus constantly gave Himself to others, spending life for them.

Mim was a grad student, a counselor in an undergraduate dormitory. Her eyes were failing her badly; she could read only a few minutes at a time. Yet day after day she gave herself to the girls in the dorm. She gave her eyes to read Scriptures with them. When migraine headaches struck, she lay on a sofa, propped up with pillows, and opened her door to welcome any who might come. She was laying down her life for others. She was loving as Jesus loves. You and I may never be called on to die for our brothers. But we *are* called on to give our lives daily for them.

(2) *Accepting from others* (v. 14). Have you ever thought how amazing it is that God, who with a word formed our vast universe, who with a touch can give sight to the blind or life to the dead, lets *us* minister to *Him?* And yet He does so. He could do it so much easier without us, but He accepts our pitiful efforts and gives us praise for them (cf. 1 Cor. 4:5).

This is how to see Jesus' commands. Not as the brutal demands of a harsh master, but as the loving invitation of a God who stoops to let His friends minister to Him.

Often "being ministered to" is hard for us. We

want to be on the giving end (where we feel secure or even proud), but not on the receiving end (where we may feel obligated or even ashamed). A mother I knew constantly tried to tie her children to her by money gifts. But she could not be a "gracious receiver." She had to give and would not receive.

But real love humbles itself and accepts the gifts of others. For you and me, this may mean admitting need (personal or spiritual) and letting a brother minister encouragement and help. When we love "just as" Jesus loves, we accept and welcome the ministry of our brothers.

(3) *Sharing ourselves* (v. 15). A slave follows his master's orders blindly. The master does not share motives or feelings or reasons with a slave. He *uses* the slave, as one might use a tool or appliance.

Jesus guarded against any such misunderstanding of the word "command" (v. 14). Believers minister to Him as friends, not slaves.

In His love, Jesus opened up His life to His friends. He told them "everything" that He had heard from His father. There were no masks in this relationship, no hidden motives, no secret plans. Jesus invited His disciples to know Him and share all He was and is.

When we love others as Jesus, we open up our lives to them as He did. We let them see us as we are. We take off the masks and let our brothers share our lives.

Sometimes this is hard because we're not all we

want to be. We're afraid that others will judge us or fail to respect us if they see our weaknesses.

I was always afraid in my marriage to share my weaknesses or problems. Soon I found it hard to share positive things as well. We only talked of ideas and superficial things. We didn't really *know* each other. And after 10 years of marriage I was shocked to hear my wife say she knew I didn't love her! Finally I learned that, to communicate love, a person has to share himself honestly with others. Sharing ourselves is a vital part of "just as" love.

(4) *Choosing to love* (v. 16). Often friendships grow when two persons find they like each other. Sometimes friendships are formed for mutual benefit (as when one ardent fisherman has a boat, and another an outboard motor). Even "love" works this way. She loves him because he is such a good provider.

But Jesus' love is given by an act of will. He chose to love us, even when we were yet sinners. It's natural to respond to someone who loves us. But Christlike love isn't based on such feelings or on what we will get out of a relationship. *Jesus chose to love us*. And to love as Jesus does means that we choose to love our brothers. This kind of love, by choice rather than feeling, is a trustworthy, constant love on which we can depend.

Wouldn't it be good to know that others love you that way? Unconditionally. That no matter what, your brothers *care?* This is the kind of love we're to know in Christ's Church.

(5) *Helping brothers grow* (v. 16). Jesus reas-

sured His disciples. His love would not leave them unchanged. He had chosen them to bear fruit. He would make them productive.

It's exciting to realize. Jesus commits Himself to nurturing us to productivity.

This too is a way we are to live love with others. So often our relationships are superficial. We talk about our children, our plans, our trips. But how often do we share our experiences in the Lord? How often do we talk about some fresh thing Jesus has done for us, some new insight from the Word? How often do we encourage each other or stimulate each other to a closer walk with the Lord? But this is part of Jesus' "just as" kind of love. We are to encourage each other, to build each other up in Christ. How vital then that love lead us to focus our relationships with our brothers on our common Lord.

(6) *Remaining open* (v. 16). A believer can cut himself off from God by turning aside from His ways for a time. But God does not cut Himself off from the believer. "Come boldly," the Bible reminds us, "unto the throne of grace" in time of need (Heb. 4:16, av). Jesus' love guarantees us access to the Father. He tells us, "Ask the Father in My name."

Loving one another as Jesus loves us means that we cannot cut ourselves off from one another. A fellow Christian may hurt us or sin against us. It's so easy then to put up the barriers, to hide behind a mask. But this isn't Jesus' "just as" love. We're to always welcome a brother and hold firm to our love for him.

(7) *Responding freely* (v. 16). God's love is so amazing. When we come to Him, He responds to us! Jesus' deep desire is that we might always remain close to Him, that God might answer our prayers. For, Jesus promises, the Father *will* listen and answer prayer in Jesus' name.

Loving with Jesus' love means that we too will be sensitive and respond freely to each other. So often we talk *at* each other. We say and hear words, but we don't look beneath them to the feelings and needs others are trying to express. Often we're so bound up in our own thoughts or feelings that we don't even try to understand another's needs.

It was only when Carol broke into tears that Marilyn realized how she felt. The girls had just been involved in an argument, each defending her own position and actions in a recent spat. Then suddenly Carol crumbled and began to cry. In her tears she shared some of the pressures that troubled her home and expressed how discouraged and hopeless she felt. At last Marilyn understood the inner pain Carol was feeling. Jumping up, she rushed over to embrace her and cry with her.

Love cares how other people feel. Love reaches out in sensitive response to them. Love listens for what's inside a person and is eager to touch and heal.

When we Christians stop to listen to each other, to understand each other's needs and feelings, and to respond with warm concern, we're living in "just as" love.

Loving as Jesus loves means experiencing God's

own love in our relationships with each other. It means constantly showing that we value and care for one another as persons . . . not because of what is done to "earn" acceptance.

How do we let others know that they are loved this way, unconditionally, for themselves?

1. We live our lives for each other.

2. We let others help us.

3. We share our real selves.

4. We love consistently, not because of how another acts or responds.

5. We focus in our relationships on helping each other grow in Christ.

6. We welcome and remain open to others.

7. We respond freely to each other.

In these ways we open lives to the ministry of God the Holy Spirit. In these ways God works through love to transform us.

GO ON GROWING IN IT

Love is to be a growing thing in the fellowship of Christians. Because love is the deepest need of every person, and because love alone can open us up to growth and change and freedom, God's Word is clear: "Above all else, cherish intense love for one another" (1 Peter 4:8).

This kind of love is supernatural, not natural. It isn't something we can give in our own strength. No human love can set aside the differences that divide people and cause us to open our hearts to our brothers. Only God's love is big enough.

How good to know that Jesus Himself lives in the heart of those who know Him as Saviour! How good to realize that Jesus wants to live His own life out through us. And so how good to turn to Christ in abandonment and cry, "O Lord, I cannot love. Teach me love. Lord, love my brothers . . . Your brothers . . . through me."

QUEST 1

Bible passages to study

1 Corinthians 13:1-10
Ephesians 4:25-32
Colossians 3:8-17

Each passage above explores ways Christians live love with each other. Study them and write down answers to the following:

What is love?

In how many ways in these passages is love expressed?

How would a person in this kind of fellowship know he was loved?

QUEST 2

Personal application

Love's way

In what ways have you experienced love from fellow Christians?

In what ways (specifically) have you shown love to your fellow believers?

From your study, what do you most need to ask God to do in your life if you are to build loving relationships?

6

With Wide Open Hearts

Some of the most tragic words in Scripture were uttered by a cripple who for 38 years had lain alone by the pool of Bethesda, hoping for healing. When Jesus noticed him, He asked, "Do you want to get well? And the man replied, "I have no one, Sir, to put me into the bathing pool right after it has been disturbed" (John 5:6, 7).

I have no one.

To everyone who has felt the ache of loneliness and the desolation that invades us when we feel no one cares, Jesus makes a simple offer. "Come to Me all ye who labor and are heavily burdened, and I will give you rest. Take My yoke upon you and learn of Me, for I am gentle and humble of heart, and you will find rest for your souls; for My yoke is easy, and My burden is light" (Matt. 11:28-30).

The yoke was a familiar thing to the men and women of Jesus' day. The shaped and smoothed wood was slipped over the shoulders to distribute the weight of water or wood, making it easier to carry. The yoke was not to increase, but to lighten loads. And a two-man yoke, distributing the load between them, made work even lighter. How deeply Jesus' words must have appealed to lonely, burdened, or guilt-ridden men. You have a heavy burden? Mine is light. So here's My yoke; let Me share your load.

Willingness to share others' burdens is uncommon. Our natural response is more like that of the elders of Israel when Judas, after the arrest of Jesus, returned the bribe he had accepted. "I sinned in betraying innocent blood," he said. They replied, "What is that to us? You see to that yourself" (Matt. 27:3, 4).

How often we feel that people will treat us that way:

"What is your problem to us? See to it yourself."

Yes, we all know how it feels to cry out, as did the lonely cripple, "I have no one."

But this is *not* to be our experience as Christians. Jesus' offer of His yoke holds firm. God's way is to lighten our loads by distributing them. When we share our burdens with our brothers, Jesus Himself also shoulders and lifts our burdens. And so the Bible says, "Carry one another's burden and thus fulfill the law of Christ" (Gal. 6:2). The way of love that we are to follow requires us to open our hearts to each other—in all that an open heart implies.

DEEPLY MOVED

One sign of an open heart is that it is moved by the needs and concerns of others. One day a leper came to Jesus, "begging of Him on his knees, 'If You are willing, You can cleanse me.' Deeply sympathetic, He reached out His hand and touched him, and said to him, 'I am willing. Be cleansed.'"

(Mark 1:40-42). Jesus was moved not only by the man's physical need. He was moved by his loneliness, for a leper was "untouchable," one whom no other person would receive. In deep sympathy, Jesus reached out to touch as well as heal . . . one of the few times when His healing was not accomplished by word alone.

Often I've felt compelled to turn away from scenes of suffering in missionary films. Somehow it hurts too much. It's easier to isolate myself from awareness of people's needs and to justify withdrawal by reminders that there seems nothing I can do to help anyway. But this is not the way of Jesus, to close our hearts to others. Instead we're to open our hearts—even to hurts and sufferings—to reach out, to touch, to care.

This is the way of life for the Church as the New Testament sketches it. "Whoever possesses the world's resources and notices that his brother is in need and then locks his heart against him, how is the love of God in him?" (1 John 3:17) Love is an utterly practical lifting of the brother's burden, sharing with him all we are and have. And so we read, "The host of believers were one in heart and soul: no one claimed his belongings just for himself, but everything was theirs in common" (Acts 4:32).

What's important here is not the particular way in which financial resources were shared. Or even the fact that each passage quoted above speaks of belongings. What is important is to see the attitude of these brothers in Christ. They were of one heart and soul. They shared. They unlocked and opened their hearts to each other.

There are numerous ways in which an attitude of deep sympathy and concern for one another is expressed. The Apostle Paul pleaded with believers as brothers, "that you strive together with me in your prayers" (Rom. 15:30). The writer of Hebrews encourages, "Do not be negligent in showing hospitality. . . . Keep in mind those who are in prison as if you are in prison with them, and the ill-treated as though you are suffering physically yourselves" (Heb. 13:2, 3). The Bible even says that God has arranged us in the body of Christ "that the members may have the same concern one for another. When one member suffers, all the members share the suffering. When a member is honored, they all share the joy" (1 Cor. 12:25, 26).

And so we're not alone.

We're linked in one body, brothers and sisters in Christ's Church, yoked to Christ and to each other in an open-hearted fellowship of love.

This is what we need to experience today. This is what we need in order to *be* the Church. We need to cry and laugh more quickly with each other. We need to give strong sympathy, letting our brothers know that none need ever say, "I have no one." For we have Christ, and we have each other.

WHEN WE'RE TROUBLED

If it's hard for us to open our hearts to feel with a brother in his troubles, it's even harder to share when *we* are troubled. Yet, this too is implied in the fellowship of the yoke, and in God's command, "Carry one another's burden" (Gal. 6:2). We can lift another's burdens only when he tells us what they are. And he can lift ours only when we reveal ourselves to him.

Many things hinder us in our attempts to let others know us and how we really feel. Maybe in our childhood we were trained to keep our feelings inside. Our parents always controlled their emotions; we seldom saw them rejoice or show affection or cry or sag in dejection. So we learned to suppress our emotions, to hide our thoughts and feelings. It's hard for a person brought up like this to learn that he doesn't have to carry the burden alone, that he can express his inner self and others will care.

Or it may be fear that keeps us from opening our lives to others—fear of rejection. "What is that to us? You see to it yourself," is a response we've all experienced. I remember how hurt I was in seventh grade when a teacher rejected a term paper I'd worked on. When I went to share my disappointment, she brutally condemned me for plagiarism of which I hadn't been aware. It hurt so much, too much to show, and far too much to ever risk the pain again. So I can understand those who fear to open up their lives to others. The risk of possible rejection seems too great.

Another thing that moves us to hide ourselves is shame. We try so hard to have others look up to us. And when they do, when we have their respect, we wonder what they'd think of us if they knew that we have problems too? If they discovered that at times our marriages know strain, our love for God flickers low, our disappointments overwhelm. It's so easy to try to hide from others what God knows so well: that we are sinners even while we're saints, that we stand in constant need of Christ to forgive and to live through us, that our human weaknesses tinge and taint the best we do. If we took our theology seriously, we might not be so hesitant to let others see us as we are . . . imperfect yet, but in the process of being transformed by the Holy Spirit. We might not let pretense, motivated by shame, cut us off from being real with others and make us hypocrites.

Then there are the "good" motives for hiding ourselves and our needs from our brothers. Sometimes we tell ourselves, "I don't want to burden others." Or we think, *He has so many troubles of his own. How can I add to them?* And we draw back and turn within ourselves. We forget that God has *commanded* "Carry one another's burden." Thinking that we understand better than He, we injure both ourselves and our brothers. For the shared burden is lighter to both!

Against all our excuses and our reasonings, God's Word speaks clearly. "Open wide your hearts." The Apostle Paul knew what he was asking. He wrote to the Corinthians, a church that was divided into factions, a church that at times mounted resistance to his authority. And always he spoke to them openly and honestly, sharing his innermost self. "O Corinthians," he says, "we address you frankly with wide-open hearts. . . . In exchange—I am speaking as to children—open wide your hearts in the same way" (2 Cor. 6:11-13).

Paul presents himself as a model of how believers ought to share with each other: frankly, with complete openness. And this is the way he lived. Paul had been forced to leave Thessalonica by persecution shortly after founding the church there. Cut off from the believers, he was disturbed by fears of what might happen to this young, uninstructed fellowship. Finally, shaken by the uncertainty, "when I could no longer stand it, I sent to make sure about your faith, whether perhaps the tempter might have tempted you" (1 Thes. 3:5). Receiving the report that they were standing fast in the Lord, Paul was filled with joy. "How can we ever repay God with enough thanksgiving for you in view of all the happiness we are enjoying because of you in the presence of our God?" (1 Thes. 3:9)

Explaining to the Corinthians that receiving God's comfort in trouble and distress equips the believer to minister encouragement to others who have similar troubles, Paul reveals his own weaknesses. Even though this church was even then questioning his apostolic authority, Paul resisted the temptation to pretend strength and instead wrote, "We want you to know, brothers, about the trouble that came to us in Asia, how we were weighed down beyond all possible endurance, so that we really despaired of life" (2 Cor. 1:8). In everything Paul did, he refused to hide behind pretense. In everything, Paul denounced "underhanded ways of which one should be ashamed," and he was always careful that he did not "behave crafti-ly, nor . . . falsify the word of God" (2 Cor. 4:2). Paul was honest with himself and others. He opened his heart wide. And God used him.

We have to resist the temptation to hide our-selves from others. We have to remember that one person Jesus couldn't touch and change was the Pharisee, whose life was built on pretense. Life with our brothers in Christ . . . the life of oneness in the Spirit . . . demands open hearts.

In opening ourselves to others, we experience the kind of love that Jesus has for us: accepting love, forgiving love, caring love. When we take this yoke, to bear one another's burdens by caring about them and letting them care for us, we begin to live together in the Spirit's oneness.

WELDED TOGETHER IN LOVE

Open-hearted love breaks through the isolation from others we've all known. Thus we can be "welded together in love, to attain all the riches that the full assurance of insight brings, with a knowl-edge of Christ, the secret of God" (Col. 2:2, 3).

Scripture gives many insights into the basic atti-tude toward others that opens hearts and builds unity. Philippians 2 contains one of the most graphic. There Paul, expressing God's own concern, exhorts, "Make my joy complete by being in agree-ment, having the same love, being united in spirit, having the same attitude" (v. 2).

How is this possible? In only one way. "Doing nothing out of selfishness or conceit, but with hu-mility regarding others as superior to yourselves.

Neither must each be looking out only for his own interests but also for those of others. Let this mind be in you which was also in Christ Jesus, who, though existing in the form of God, did not consider His equality with God something to cling to, but emptied Himself as He took on the form of a slave, and became like human beings. So, recognized in appearance as a human being, He humbled Himself, and became obedient to death; yes, death by the cross" (Phil. 2:3-8).

It is humbling to "look out for" the interests of others, becoming their servants, even as Jesus emptied Himself and took on the form of a slave. And it's humbling to share ourselves honestly with others, to let them know us with all our pretense stripped away. But we are Jesus' brothers. He did not cling to His equality with God; He became human. And we cannot cling to the shreds of our pride. "Therefore [because in Christ we have been created in God's likeness] laying all falsehood aside, speak truth each person to his neighbor, for we are one another's members" (Eph. 4:25). So too, "as God's chosen . . . clothe yourselves with tenderness of heart, kindliness, humility, gentleness, patient endurance. Bear with one another and forgive each other in case one has a grievance against another. Just as the Lord has forgiven you, so do you. But crown it all with love, which is the perfect bond of union. And let the peace of Christ, to which you were called in one body, arbitrate in your hearts. And be thankful" (Col. 3:12-15).

QUEST 1

Bible passages to study

Colossians 3:1-15

How is it possible for us to live with each other in Christ's way?

What attitudes toward others and toward ourselves does the way of life we reject imply?

What is the "new self" like?

What evidence does this passage contain that Christ's way of living with other demands openness?

Philippians 2:1-11

What makes it possible for us to have unity with other Christians?

What attitudes toward ourselves are key to "being united in the spirit?"

What central attitude did Christ exhibit, and why is this basic to unity?

What is the end of the pathway Jesus followed?

What does this suggest for us?

QUEST 2

Personal application

Empathy

Name the others you know well enough to "feel with" in problems or joys.

How have you come to know them so well?

How have you tried to "bear their burdens?"

Openness

Name others who know you well enough to "feel with" you in problems or joys.

How have they come to know you so well?

What is the most difficult thing for you in trying
   to be open with others?
List any burdens you may feel just now that you
   need help to bear.

7

Agree in the Lord

There were times when Ross enjoyed the annual
meeting, times when he and the other members of
Elmdale Bible Church rejoiced together, praising
the Lord for His working in them the past year,
and rededicating themselves for the year ahead.
And then there were times like these.

Ross knew the conflict over the new gymnasium
would carry over from the board to the congregational meeting. Charlie Hill had been dead set
against the gym idea from the first. Unreasonably
so. And the fact that all the others lined up against
him only seemed to anger him and make him more
stubborn.

When the board's recommendation to go ahead
with the addition was made at the annual meeting,
Ross expected Charlie to present his "minority
view." But he hadn't expected the bitter outburst,
the accusations, and the deep-seated antagonism
that poured out. Nor had he expected Harvey to

react, exploding with an answering hostility against Charlie. The others had reacted too, taking sides in the conflict, expressing the same anger that he had been surprised to sense in himself and had struggled to contain.

Finally the chairman adjourned the meeting, but not before the harm had been done. Now Ross, at home, looked up a verse he wished he had remembered earlier that evening: "My dear brothers, let everyone be quick to listen, slow to talk, slow to get angry; for man's anger does not promote God's righteousness" (James 1:19). And Ross remembered another verse, something Paul had written to two feuding women, "I appeal to (you) to agree in the Lord" (Phil. 4:2). How, Ross wondered, when conflicts come so suddenly and flared so hotly, can we learn to "agree in the Lord?"

We've all known conflicts between believers within the church. Some have been silly: a misunderstanding, blown out of proportion by gossip and second-hand reports. Some have been tragic: two elders of the church who have known and prayed with each other for years differ; bitterness grows, and then months or years of not speaking follow. Some conflicts split churches: a dispute over the calling of a pastor, a disagreement over the best way to reach a common goal, that suddenly takes an overwhelming importance and divides brother from brother.

Whatever the cause, or the motivations of those involved, conflict does break the unity of the body of Christ, and keeps those who are brothers and sisters from experiencing oneness in the Spirit.

73

Surely the God who said, "agree in the Lord," gives us some insights in His word that help us understand conflict and how to respond to it. God must have revealed ways to work out our conflicts with others, ways that permit us to maintain, and even deepen, our essential oneness in Christ.

CONFLICT

Conflict in itself isn't unhealthy. Most marriage counselors agree, for instance, that *solving* conflicts strengthens a marriage. It isn't the disagreement that is destructive. It's how a couple reacts to disagreement that creates problems.

It's the same in any interpersonal relationships. People do differ. Misunderstandings arise. Feelings are hurt. Anger and bitterness and competitiveness well up in us, causing us to strike out at each other. It's this pattern of relationships, not disagreement, that is destructive and wrong. And so the Bible directs our attention away from the issues to the response of believers who disagree and their resulting relationship with each other.

"Who among you is wise and understanding? Let him show by his good behavior that his actions are carried on with unobtrusive wisdom. But if you cherish bitter jealousy and rivalry in your hearts, do not pride yourself in this and play false to the truth. Such wisdom does not come down from above; instead it is earthly, unspirited, demonic, for where jealousy and rivalry exist, there will be confusion and everything base. But the wisdom from above is first of all pure, then peaceable, courteous, congenial, full of mercy and good fruits, impartial and sincere. And the harvest, which righteousness yields to the peacemakers, comes from a sowing in peace" (James 3:13-18). God's wisdom avoids divisive conflict and seeks a peaceful way to resolve issues and differences.

It's striking to see, as James moves on in this discussion, asking, "Where do conflicts and fightings among you originate?" (James 4:1), that he never intimates that conflict comes from the issues involved. Instead we read, "Do they not spring from your passions that are at war in your members? You covet and do not have; you murder and strive and cannot attain; you fight and battle, and do not possess" (James 4:1, 2). So the first thing to grasp in dealing with conflict is this: the battlefield is often *within us* . . . not in the things over which we clash. Somehow battles like those between Charlie Hill and the rest of the church board over the new gymnasium can't be solved by deciding who is right. The very anger and hostility which mark the conflict is clear evidence that it is the persons, not the reasons or issues, that have become central. To agree in the Lord we need to apply God's pure, peaceable, and courteous wisdom to dealing with the people who disagree over the issue.

FOCUS ON PEOPLE

When we realize that the battlefield is within, specifically in the hearts of the *others* in the conflict, it's easy to fall into the trap of passing judgment. Yet we can't be quick to condemn or blame others, even those whom we feel are acting most unreasonably or unlovingly. Scripture says, "Do not pass judgment," and so Christ Himself cuts us off from the easy way of blaming others for the difficulty. "Why notice the splinter in your brother's eye without taking notice of the beam in your own eye?" Christ continues. "You hypocrite! First get rid of that beam in your eye; then you will see clearly to extract the splinter from your brother's eye" (Matt. 7:1-5).

Why did Charlie Hill break out in anger at the congregational meeting? Why did he feel that the whole board was against him? Why did the board go on talking about the gym without stopping to help a brother who was obviously upset? If the men had paused to show concern for Charlie and a desire to understand his feelings and viewpoint, likely the flare-up at the church would never have happened.

We can't blame others for conflict. We have to look at ourselves. "Did I accept his feelings and viewpoints? Did he sense that I cared, deeply, when he became upset?" This is the kind of question we need to address—to ourselves.

We're all subject to rising feelings of anger. Scripture suggests this in itself isn't always sin (Eph. 4:26). It may quickly lead to sin, however, so we're to deal with our anger and see that it doesn't remain to corrode and corrupt fellowship.

All these principles will not, in themselves, resolve our conflicts. But they are first principles. Love, don't condemn, your brother. Help, don't judge, him. Don't react in man's competitive and self-righteous way. Respond with God's own peaceable and courteous concern. Deal with anger.

But with this said, we must go on to explore types of conflicts that call for specific responses ... conflicts that involve us with injured people, with selfish people, and with sinning people.

Injured people. It had been a silly remark. Sylvia hadn't really meant it. But she saw the hurt look in Carolyn's eyes. Of course, Sylvia had quickly dismissed the matter. If Carolyn was foolish enough to take it seriously, that was her problem. How could Carolyn even think that Sylvia had meant it *that* way?

Many things we do, some unconsciously or thoughtlessly, hurt others and may lead to conflict. How will Carolyn react now? Probably it will depend on her personality. Some of us hide our hurts deep inside where they lie and ache unhealed. We try to hide the hurt from others and even to pretend that everything is the same between us and the person who hurt us. But the pain is still there, and we can't feel close to them or trust them any more.

Others strike out when hurt. They fight back, and try to hurt those who injure them. This kind of person may gossip and so take revenge. Or this kind may strike out openly, face to face, but usually attacking over some issue that has nothing to do with the original hurt. This is what Carolyn did. At a women's auxiliary meeting three weeks after Sylvia's remark, Carolyn bitterly attacked the way Sylvia had run the women's part of the annual missionary conference. Sylvia had to admit there was some basis for her criticism. But the antagonism of the attack made it plain that Sylvia's planning was not the real cause of the conflict.

After the meeting, Sylvia kept thinking of the earlier incident and recalled the feeling she'd had then that she should apologize to Carolyn. A basic Bible principle applied, a principle that Jesus stated: "When you are offering your gift at the altar and remember that your brother holds something against you, leave your gift there at the altar and go and become reconciled to your brother; then come and offer your gift (Matt. 5:23,24). How striking a priority Christ gives to reconciliation! It comes before worship!

Now, finally, Sylvia decided to follow Jesus' way. She went to Carolyn, and humbly, with no mention of the afternoon's emotional meeting, apologized for the hurt she had caused by her thoughtless remark. The apology opened the dam of Carolyn's deep hurt, and helped Carolyn apologize for that afternoon, for a bitterness Carolyn herself hadn't realized she felt until it spilled out at the meeting.

Several guidelines for dealing with hurts and injuries that, unless healed, will cause conflict and division in the fellowship, are illustrated in this incident. First, the one who injures another needs to take the initiative in reconciliation. If you know someone "has something against you," go to him—immediately. Don't wait for him to come to you. Second, reconciliation involves both apology and forgiveness. The Bible tells us that we are to forgive one another as God for Christ's sake has forgiv-

78

en us (Eph. 4:32). None of us dares forget that he too sins and falls short. We can't afford to be proud, unwilling to admit our mistakes, unwilling to receive or extend forgiveness. God sets a pattern for maintaining harmony by telling us to confess our sins to Him and promising forgiveness and cleansing (1 John 1:9). It's this pattern we are to follow with each other (cf. Luke 17:3, 4).

Selfish people. Being a Christian doesn't free us from our old drives and desires. We still feel the urge to compete with our brothers, to be "first." This was at the heart of a dispute between the disciples. James and John had their mother ask Jesus for the chief places in His coming kingdom. And the Bible says, "When the ten heard it, they were indignant at the two brothers" (Matt. 20:24).

It was on this occasion (cf. also Luke 22:24-27) that Jesus gently told His friends, "You know that the rulers of the Gentiles lord it over them, and their superiors oppress them, but with you it is different: Whoever among you wants to be great must be your servant, and whoever would be first will be your slave, just as the Son of Man did not come to be served but to serve, and to give His life a ransom for many" (Matt. 20:24-28).

Remembering that we're not to judge others, it's clear that the first principle we note here applies to ourselves. Often we'll *feel competitive* as a prelude to, or a part of, growing conflict. When we do, we need to judge ourselves. We're not to strive to "win" a dispute or to "come out on top." We are to serve.

Roger Balis and Helen Loftus were both superintendents of Sunday School departments. Both were cramped for space. And each honestly felt that he ought to have the larger room that Helen's primaries now occupied. What began as an honest difference motivated by concern for children developed into serious conflict . . . not over the room itself, but because neither was willing to "give in" and see the other "win."

They had fallen into that "bitter jealousy and rivalry" that James warns against and had forgotten that each was to live as the servant of the other. There's only one remedy for competition, and that is for each person to seek to serve the other and solve the problem by working together in love.

What about persons who simply will not accept the servant role? The Bible describes them as "grumblers, complaining of their lot, who go along in accord with their passions, and whose mouths give vent to arrogant remarks, while they flatter to one's face in hope of gain" (Jude 16). There is no way we can force contentious people to accept the servant role that Jesus assigned to believers. But we can avoid being pulled into their ways. The Bible says, "A slave of the Lord must not quarrel: instead, he must be affable toward everyone, skilled in teaching, willing to suffer wrong. In a gentle way he must correct those who put themselves in opposition to him" (2 Tim. 2:24, 25).

What if there is still no response? Then, Paul says "to keep an eye on those who cause divisions and temptations, quite out of harmony with the doctrine you have been taught, and to keep away from them. For people of that type do not serve our Lord Christ but their own appetites" (Rom. 16:17).

It may be hard to tell for sure just when to apply one of these principles to specific cases. But in general we can say this: When we feel competitive, it's time to remember we are our brothers' servant. When we see another person acting competitively or arrogantly, we need to guard against being drawn into a quarrel, and to gently correct and minister to him. If a person continuously and characteristically causes divisions, then as a group of believers we are to "keep away from him."

Sinning people. Jesus' command not to judge others is directed at our habit of imputing motives and attitudes. "He's just angry because he lost the election," or, "He must be out of fellowship with the Lord to even *think* of going there!" are the kind of judgments that the Bible clearly rules out (cf. Romans 14:2-4).

But the Bible also tells us that we *are* to judge overt sin. "If a pretended brother is immoral or greedy or idolatrous or abusive or a drinker or a robber, you must not associate with him, nor even eat with one of that type" (1 Cor. 5:11). The passage is even more explicit: "Expel that wicked person from your own company" (5:13).

The response of expulsion seems harsh to some. Actually it is meant as a ministry to the sinning brother. Sin warps his life as well as that of others, and it brings him into deep unhappiness. The withdrawal of fellowship is designed to restore the brother, for rejection by God's family hurts the

81

true child of God and may lead him to repentance and restoration.

If we are to have harmony in the church, we must have discipline and deal with overt sin before inevitable conflict and dissension arise.

TOWARD AGREEMENT

Our first concern when conflict arises is always to be for the persons involved. This is not to suggest that the issues are unimportant. (In fact, in the next chapter we'll see how the issues are to be resolved.) *But we can make no real progress in working out problems if we do not approach them in a spirit of unity and oneness.*

Realizing that much conflict comes from within persons (and not from our differences over the issues), we can examine our responses to others with whom we differ, and we can deal in God's way with the hurts, the motives, and the sin that turns disagreement into warfare. When we face our differences together, in love, as those who are privileged to serve one another, we have a basis for seeking agreement on the issues.

QUEST 1

Bible passages to study
Acts 6:1-7
Galatians 2:11-21
How, in each case, did the conflict arise?
What principles discussed in the chapter are illustrated.
Are there any additional principles suggested?

Personal application

Conflict

Write a brief description of the last time you were involved in a conflict with another.

What principles discussed in this chapter seem most applicable to the case you have described?

How might you have acted on these principles?

What relationship(s) with others *right now* might be improved by acting on one or more of these principles? Describe.

8

One Heart and Mind

Being of one heart always comes before being of one mind.

Thus Paul prays for his brothers that "their hearts may be encouraged, welded together in love" in order that they might "attain all the riches that the full assurance of insight brings, with a knowledge of Christ" (Col. 2:2). Loving each other opens up our lives to the ministry of the Holy Spirit, freeing us to grow and change and learn. Lack of love closes us off to each other . . . and to God.

We can see why.

When Ann met Mark, she immediately felt that she wanted to marry him. But she couldn't believe he could ever care for her. So whenever they were together, Ann was careful to act and say the things she felt he would like, rather than share what she herself thought or felt. Actually, Ann was wrong about Mark's interest in her. He had been immediately attracted to her and sensed the possibility of love. But as they continued to date, Ann would never let him know what she liked and wanted to do. When he asked, it was always, "Whatever you say," or "What do you want to do?" At first it had been great for Mark, being with someone who seemed to enjoy whatever he planned and think what he thought. But later, with the awareness that he didn't really know Ann, doubts and frustration came.

Ann's attitude—her inability to believe that Mark could love or accept her as she was—eventually led him to break off the relationship. Her closed life convinced him they could never grow to oneness.

Oneness, in marriage or in the Christian's relationship in the Spirit with his brothers and sisters, is something we grow into. It begins with the assurance that we are accepted and valued. Knowing we are loved, we are freed to open our hearts and share with one another. And in thus coming to know each other better, love and understanding grow, and oneness becomes a thing of the heart *and* mind.

It's important to get this sequence clear, for it

helps us identify three "stages" of love that lead to the kind of unity in which we can solve the problems that otherwise become occasions for conflict.

The sequence, and the "stages" of love involved, are:

1. *Accepting love:* Oneness begins when we accept one another as brothers and love each other for Jesus' sake.

2. *Expressive love:* Knowing we love and are loved by our brothers frees us to open our lives to each other and share our true selves.

3. *Personalized love:* As we come to know and understand each other better, we grow to love each other as unique individuals.

4. *Unity of mind:* Experiencing all three stages of love, we grow in time to unity of mind concerning important matters that relate to God's will.

BREAKDOWN

Now perhaps we can better see why unity of mind so often escapes us in our churches. Often we begin well, with the first kind of love. But we fail to move to love's second stage. As in Ann's relationship with Mark, we really do care. But somehow we can't find the courage to open up our lives to each other. And so our growth is blocked, short of knowing and loving each other as individuals.

Love that stops short like this is a half-way love. And half-way love easily turns sour. When we try to hold our fellowships together merely by asserting our relationship in Christ without going on to deepening and personalizing our love, disagreement often becomes conflict. And the feelings we develop for each other as individuals become those of anger and suspicion and rivalry ... all very far from the "love" we insist we still have. And so that old saying, "I love my brother, but I don't like him," is shown up as a fraud. It is a clear indication of halfway love. And Jesus' command permits no halfway measures: "Love one another," He said, "*just as* I have loved you."

For Ann the way to let love grow would have been to take the risk of self-revelation, to let Mark know her as she really was. For believers this is also the way to help love grow toward true unity: sharing ourselves with one another, coming to know each other as individuals. Really, this isn't as great a risk as it may seem. For we *are* one in Christ. God loves us as individuals. And as His other children, our brothers, come to know us as He does, His Spirit creates in their hearts a reflection of His love for us.

WHOSE MIND?

How can we really solve the problems that every fellowship of Christians faces? Should we build a new addition? Is this the right candidate to call as our pastor? How are we going to try to reach our community for Christ? Should we go to cottage prayer meetings in homes instead of the weekly meeting at church? What is the real purpose of our Sunday evening service, and how are we going to achieve it? Should the teaching of the Bible be through lecture or by discussion?

These and many other questions call for decisions. How are we going to make these decisions?

How are we going to "be of one mind" on issues where there are varying points of view?

The principles we've explored to this point clear the way for an understanding of the ultimate basis on which we as Christians reach agreement. We *prepare* for decision by dealing with conflict on an interpersonal level, making sure that we maintain harmony and mutual love (chapter 7). We have a *context* for decision when we are of unified heart, experiencing a full love that has grown through coming to know each other and to care for each other as individuals. When conflict has been dealt with and a climate of love developed, then we are ready to consider decision.

And our decisions are reached by realizing that the only basis for any action regarding Christ's Church is Jesus' will.

In one place the Bible says a striking thing. "We have the mind of Christ" (1 Cor. 2:16). And in another, "Let this mind be in you which was also in Christ Jesus" (Phil. 2:5). These verses speak an astonishing truth. *We can let Jesus Christ make our decisions.*

Most of us realize that this is true for individuals. We speak of "God's leading." We pray and ask God to direct us when we're choosing a college or a wife or making some other decision. But we haven't taken seriously enough the truth that, just as Christ directs and guides individuals, He also directs the life of His body, the Church.

Many passages of Scripture point out that Jesus Christ is the living Head of His Church. "God has placed everything under His feet and has given

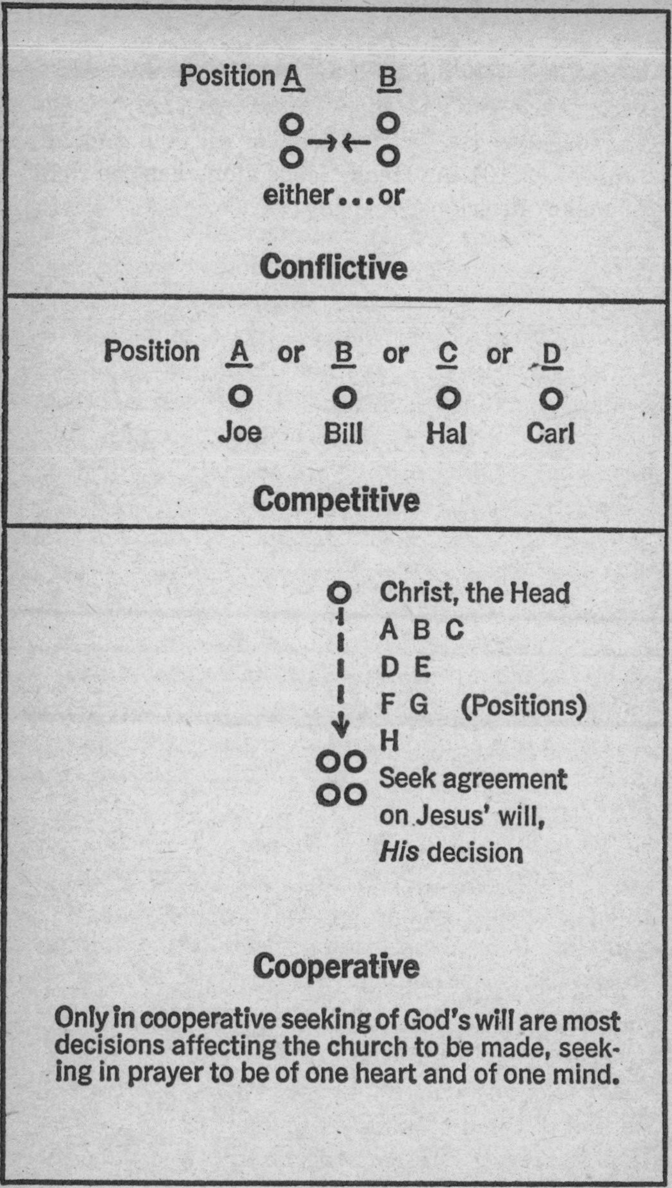

Position <u>A</u>   <u>B</u>

O →← O
O   O

either ... or

Conflictive

Position <u>A</u> or <u>B</u> or <u>C</u> or <u>D</u>

O   O   O   O
Joe   Bill   Hal   Carl

Competitive

O   Christ, the Head
    A B C
    D E
    F G   (Positions)
    H
OO Seek agreement
OO on Jesus' will,
    His decision

Cooperative

Only in cooperative seeking of God's will are most decisions affecting the church to be made, seeking in prayer to be of one heart and of one mind.

Figure 1
Three types of decision-making

Him as head over everything for the Church, which is His body," we're told in Ephesians 1:22, 23. Colossians says, He "is the head of all rule and authority" (2:10). As Head, Jesus alone has the right to make decisions relating to the life of His Church.

Our task, then, in resolving and solving problems, is *not* to decide what is best, but to *discover the decision Jesus has already made.*

This immediately changes the whole process of decision-making.

Figure 1 shows three common methods of decision-making, two of which are ruled out when we approach decision as seeking to determine the will of God.

Conflictive decision-making takes place when two different positions dominate, and the decision is seen as an either/or choice. Recently one church came close to a split because one group insisted prayer meeting must be held Wednesday nights in the church basement for everyone, while another group insisted prayer meeting should be replaced by small groups meeting in homes at convenient times. In the rivalry and antagonism that developed, neither group was really seeking God's will. Each group had made up its mind and was involved in fighting the other.

Either/or thinking nearly always leads to conflict, cutting persons off from each other and from agreement on God's will.

Competitive decision-making is much like conflictive decision-making. It is marked by exploration of several alternatives but by a too-quick determination by individuals that this or that choice is best. When Joe and Bill and Hal and Carl have all made up their minds to support different options, each tends to seek arguments for his choice and not to listen to the points made by others. In this spirit of competition, the basic task of coming to understand and agree on God's will is forgotten.

Cooperative decision-making begins with the assumption by all that they will come to a Spirit-led agreement. To do this, they encourage the expression of different points of view and feelings. Rather than promoting a particular choice, each realizes the need to listen to and understand the others and to understand the many possible choices that open up before them.

In cooperative decision-making, then, we resist the temptation to take a position before we've examined the insights and ideas of all our brothers. Then we take time to test various possibilities by the Word of God. Finally we pray together *until we come to agreement on what is to be done*, expecting God the Holy Spirit to lead us to the decision made by Christ.

The cooperative approach, then, is marked by these things: (1) an atmosphere of mutual love and appreciation that encourages expression and acceptance of different points of view, (2) a willingness to listen to everyone's idea and feelings about the issue; (3) a commitment to talk and pray together about the decision until there is agreement on what Christ's choice for the body is.

When we realize that it is not our responsibility to "make a decision" but that we are to discover the decision Christ has made as our Head, we are on the way to becoming "of one mind" as well as "of one heart" in the Lord.

DECISIONS

The cooperative process just sketched is the Bible's basic approach to decision-making for the church. In most cases, it is the only appropriate one.

Decisions affecting the church. When any decision touches the life of the congregation or of a particular group within the congregation, it is best to seek a consensus of those involved. A consensus is agreement by those involved that a particular choice is the one that should be made at the time. And consensus can only be reached through the cooperative process.

Consensus doesn't mean that everyone is convinced a particular course is ideal. It does mean, however, that no one is "dead set" against it. Consensus means that no one says, "I cannot accept this as being God's will for us now." When Christ gives peace about a decision, His people, remembering that as members of the one body, we are all called to live in harmony (Col. 3:15), can know they are acting in His will.

Disputes between individuals. Sometimes conflict or disagreement develops between individuals. Paul reports such a case in 1 Corinthians 6, in which two believers went to law before a pagan court.

Christians are not to resort to this means for settling differences between themselves. Instead, Paul told the church to appoint competent men from the fellowship to judge such "everyday" cases. The ones acting as judges listen to both sides and seek God's will in making their determination. And the believers involved are to submit to the decision made by the brothers.

How much better to know, when you have a dispute, that those who love you both will help settle it, and not be forced to go before an impersonal court!

Decision by leaders. The Church of Christ does have leaders, men who are chosen by God and recognized by His people as knowing Christ well and following Him closely. At times (just as in marriage) decisions *must* be made where there is no agreement. In such exceptional cases, we are to submit to those who bear responsibility to God for us. Decisions by leaders will be more readily accepted when they are made in a spirit of love, as by Paul, who seldom commanded obedience, even though he might have done so as an apostle. Instead, Paul urged believers to respond out of love for Christ. When we know that a decision affecting us was made in love, with full understanding of our feelings and needs, we will be much more confident that it reflects God's will.

Now let us sum up our conclusions. Coming to one mind concerning the decisions that must be made in our churches and fellowships is an essential element of our oneness in the Spirit. In most cases the cooperative process of working toward consensus is God's way to discover Christ's will. In cases of dispute (which usually imply that one or both parties are out of the will of God and thus unable to act in harmony), Spirit-filled members of the congregation are to be appointed to judge. And in some circumstances, the responsibility of sensing the will of God falls on church leaders. As they, acting in love, report the decision which they believe to be Christ's own, members of the church are to submit as to Him.

Living together in wholehearted love, seeking together to *do* God's will in all things, we can trust the Holy Spirit to teach us and bring us to "one mind" in Christ.

QUEST 1

Bible passage to study
Philippians 1:27—2:11
What has this passage to do with decisions?
Why is there so much stress on relationships?
What specific teachings relate directly to cooperative decision-making?

QUEST 2

Personal applications
Decisions we face
Make a list of all the questions or problems on which your church needs to become of one mind.
Briefly write out an analysis of the climate in your church as facilitating or inhibiting cooperative decision-making.
What can you do to help others in your church work toward unity of mind and understanding of God's will in decisions to be made?

9

First Place

In all our thinking about oneness in our relationship as Christians, we mustn't forget that God has a purpose in making us one body. This purpose is brought into focus in Colossians, where Christ is again presented as "Head of the body, the Church." And that purpose? "That in every respect He might have first place" (Col. 1:18).

Unity is important for us, because when we are welded together in love we can help each other give Jesus Christ first place in our lives.

When Jesus first called His disciples, He told them, "Follow Me" (Matt. 4:19). He told unbelievers that they must believe in Him. And He told those who did believe that they must follow. "If anyone serves Me," Jesus said, "let him follow Me; then where I am, there also will My servant be" (John 12:26). It is our ministry in the Church of Christ to help each other stay close to Jesus.

It's exciting to realize what staying close to Jesus means for you and me. It means transformation. It means becoming more and more *like* Him . . . in our personalities, our understanding, our love, and in our lives.

The Bible stresses the theme of Christlikeness

often. God has chosen us, we read, to "become like His Son, so that His Son would be the First, with many brothers" (Rom. 8:29, LB). In many other places the Bible tells us to "be like" our heavenly Father. God has, in giving us His life, determined that His life should grow within us, and that we might become more and more like Him.

For growth in godliness, we need always to keep Christ first in our lives, following Him closely. And for keeping Christ first, we need each other.

BUILD UP ONE ANOTHER

The Bible speaks much of helping each other grow as Christians. "So let us definitely aim for everything that contributes to one another's peace and development," Paul writes (Rom. 14:19). Other passages give us hints on how we can help each other grow.

Hebrews 10:24, 25. "Let us also be mindful to stimulate one another toward love and helpful activities, not neglecting to meet together, as is habitual with some, but giving mutual encouragement and all the more so since you see the Day approaching."

1 Corinthians 14:26. "What then, brothers? When you meet together, each one contributes his part—a song, a lesson, a revelation, a tongue, an interpretation of it; everything should be constructive."

Hebrews 2:12, 13. "Look out, brothers, so that there may not be a wicked, unbelieving heart in any of you that would lead you to fall away from the living God. Instead, give daily warning to one

95

another so long as we may speak of today, so that not one of you may be hardened through the delusion of sin."

Philippians 4:8, 9. "Finally, brothers, whatever is true, whatever is honorable, whatever is just, whatever is pure, whatever is lovely, whatever is kindly spoken, whatever is lofty and whatever is praiseworthy—put your mind on these. And what you have learned and received and heard and seen in me, that put into practice. And the God of peace will be with you."

1 Thessalonians 2:8-12. "We loved you dearly— so dearly that we gave you not only God's message but our own lives too. . . . You yourselves are our witnesses—as is God—that we have been pure and honest and faultless toward every one of you. We talked to you as a father to his own children— don't you remember?—pleading with you, encouraging you and even demanding that your daily lives should not embarrass God, but bring joy to Him who invited you into His kingdom to share His glory" (LB).

And there are other passages as well that focus our attention on how, living out our oneness in the Spirit, we can build up each other and help each other keep Christ first in our lives. Specifically, what do passages like these teach us about how to help each other grow?

FOUR FACTORS

There seem to be at least four factors involved in the building process. Each operates only in a context of love, that full love we looked at in the last chapter, which has gone on from recognition of one another as brothers in Christ to knowing and caring for each other as individuals. In the fellowship of love, we help each other grow by:

1. *Gathering together.* The Bible lets us know that it is important for Christians to get together regularly (Heb. 10:25). This we all know. But the Bible describes characteristics of our gatherings that we sometimes tend to overlook. In our meetings, Scripture says, we are to "stimulate one another toward love," "give mutual encouragement," and "each one contribute his part." Clearly our gatherings are to be marked by some significant level of interaction . . . of mutual sharing. Thus Paul writes, concerning his desire to visit the church at Rome, "I am yearning to see you so that I may bestow on you some spiritual gift for your confirmation—I mean that we may be mutually strengthened by your faith and mine" (Rom. 1:11, 12). Even the great apostle did not have a "one way" ministry.

Often when a person speaks of the need for more participation by the congregation in church meetings, he is viewed as attacking the pulpit and the pastor. This isn't necessarily so. The preached Word always will have a central place in the life of the church and the pastor a central role. What is needed is balance, a blend of preaching and participation.

Too often churches today have fallen into a "one way" pattern of ministry. We come to church and sit passively through a Sunday School class. Then we sit through the morning service. We listen to the evening service. And sometimes we only listen again on prayer meeting night. Where in this pattern is the "stimulate one another" and "give mutual encouragement" and "each one contribute" that the Bible indicates is to mark gatherings of the Church?

So we need to evaluate our coming together as Christians and seek ways to develop a balanced church life. Actually, it's not too hard to do . . . many today are doing just this. How?

Sunday School classes in some churches are opening up to a discussion approach in teaching. (The *Leader's Guide* to this book has many suggestions to help class members talk over with one another the truths explored here and to help them come to know each other better.) While not all adults feel comfortable with a participation format, each church should provide such classes for those who are eager to become more involved.

Small groups of believers are increasingly forming in many churches. Often these groups meet in homes to share and pray together and to give that "mutual encouragement" the Bible says is so important for spiritual growth. Rather than resisting the formation of such groups, churches today should encourage them and help those involved learn *how* to study God's Word together and how to love each other just as Jesus loves us.*

---

*The author's book, Creative Bible Study, *is designed to help launch small group Bible studies (Zondervan, $4.95).*

How To Conduct Home Bible Classes, *Albert J. Wollen (Scripture Press, 75¢), gives practical guidance.*

Evening services in many churches are being opened up to greater participation. Patterns vary from church to church from permitting any to get up and share spontaneously with the congregation to having panels of laymen discuss issues Christians face, to holding discussions of a Bible message over coffee in the church basement or in a home after the evening service.

Sharing can take place in any service. In a church I served, we gave five minutes weekly to a brief interview with a member who had had some experience of God's grace that week. As the congregation became aware that God was really at work in our lives, all felt a growing encouragement and enthusiasm.

Christians are to gather regularly, for we do need each other to stimulate maximum growth in Christ. And when we gather, we need a blend of *receiving* the ministry of the Word and *giving* a ministry of love and encouragement.

2. *Being personally involved.* There are several indications in the verses looked at earlier in this chapter that our involvement with our brothers in Christ isn't to be just a Sunday kind of thing. "Give daily warning to one another," "pleading with you, encouraging you," and "aim for *everything* that contributes to one another's peace and development" all give insight into the way believers can build each other up in Christ.

Basic to this portrait, of course, is the fact that we are to know one another well. It's hard to imagine a young couple in love who are satisfied with meeting once or twice a week to listen together to a lecture and then to go their separate ways. Love seeks deeper involvement, to know one another better, to open hearts and lives so that growth in oneness can take place. So too in the Church of Christ, Christians are to enjoy one another's company, to keep close to each other as persons, and never slacken in interest in one another (Rom. 12:11).

We can easily evaluate our effectiveness here. Do we see each other aside from regular church meetings? Do we really know our brothers well, so that we are able to warn and encourage them in everything? Do our brothers know us and have this kind of personal ministry to us?

Barb told a few college friends of her sense of need for more prayer and Bible study. The next few days as they met on campus, each encouraged her. "How did it go today, Barb?" "What did the Lord have for you this morning?" "How's the prayer life coming, Barb?" Because she had friends who knew her needs and who cared enough to encourage her daily, Barb was helped to grow and develop in vital areas of her Christian life.

It's this kind of close, personal, stimulating, and encouraging ministry that we each need in order to follow Christ more closely and keep Him in first place in our lives.

3. *By focusing our sharing.* Often we have Christian friends . . . but lack of Christian fellowship.

You've heard it at church, at adult class socials, as two Christians chat over lunch. "We meet each other and talk about our trips and children and plans and what's happening these days at church, but we so seldom talk about Jesus and what He's doing in our lives."

Christians are to keep Christ first and to keep Christ in constant focus. We are to share out of our own growing relationship with the Lord as an encouragement to others. And it is particularly vital to encourage each other to respond to God as He speaks to us in His Word.

One cause of breakdown in the fellowship of the church is the failure to keep Christ, and our experience with Him, in focus when we meet for church business. How many church boards meet, pray, and rush immediately into problem solving? How many committees hurry to their business without stopping to share what Jesus is doing in persons' lives? When our times together lose that vital focus on Jesus Christ and His Word and drift into superficial conversations and "business only" meetings, we're unable to build each other up or help each other give Jesus first place in our lives.

4. *Being living examples.* This is the fourth, and one of the most vital, ways that we can minister to each other. More than once Paul appeals to a church he has founded and says, "Let me be your example in this," or "be imitators of me, as I am of Christ." And we see the same thrust in Philippians 4: "What you have learned and received and heard and seen in me, that put into practice. And the God of peace will be with you" (v. 9).

Actually, we are only close to Jesus (and thus growing in Him) when we are living in responsive obedience to His Word. The Bible says, "true love of God means this, that we observe His commands" (1 John 5:3), and "He who obeys His commands remains in Him and He in him" (1 John 3:24). For this reason Paul insists, "What you have heard and seen in me, *do*." Only when an individual personally responds to Jesus Christ and sets out to follow Him will he grow and develop as a Christian.

This is why it's so encouraging to have examples. We can *see* the reality of Jesus' way and Word being lived by others. We can *know* that God is trustworthy when we see Him work in the lives of others. Knowing what God has done for our brothers, we're encouraged to step out in faith, to obey God, and find Him working excitingly in our own lives.

So we face again the desperate need of Christians for one another: the need to hear from our brothers how God answers prayer, the need to see in our brothers steadfastness under trial, the need to sense in our brothers the joy of touching a life for Jesus or helping someone over a difficult barrier. When we know people who are excited about Jesus Christ and who live in daily fellowship with Him, we're motivated to go on ourselves, to follow more closely the One who has called us to be like Him.

QUEST 1

Bible passage to study
Hebrews 3:7-19
How did the Israelites respond to God's voice?

How do you think the people affected each
   other?
What is the basic reason why God's people could
   not enter the promised land?
What are the implications of verses 12, 13 and
   how can we heed this warning?

QUEST 2

Describe how another person has motivated you
   or helped you to follow Jesus?
Look over the four ways to help each other described in this chapter. For each, (a) either
   evaluate your own church's strengths and
   weaknesses or (b) plan specific ways that you
   can act to build up others.

10

In Our Church

Somehow unity seems especially hard to maintain these days. There's a spirit of change and
question in our society, and we feel it in our
churches as well. Waves of criticism of the church,
charges of irrelevance leveled by young people as
they leave us, pressures to change traditional
methods and meetings, all are producing strain.

The board chairman of a local church asked, "Is
what we're experiencing unusual, or is this kind of

thing happening across the country?" I was able to reassure him that the problems he faces are not unique. Many churches today are struggling with pressures to change, with the reactions of "traditional" and "contemporary" people to the pressures, and with uncertainty about the direction their ministry must take if they are to live in our world as Christ's Church.

Even churches that have not yet felt the tensions soon will! For today within the Church we are asking questions that were unasked just five years ago. What *is* the Church? What are the goals and functions of the local church? How can we be more effective in serving Christ in our churches? And disagreement over answers to these basic questions is reflected in tensions in many churches throughout the world.

This isn't an unhealthy or bad thing. God wants us all to examine our lives constantly and to probe together for His will. We need to examine all our thoughts and practices by God's Word and be willing to *do* God's will as He reveals it. Whatever His Spirit shows us. However He may change or confirm our current ideas and practices.

But it's difficult. It's hard to reexamine things we've been doing . . . and often been satisfied with . . . for so many years. It's hard to try to listen patiently to those who criticize us and who appear "radical." It's hard for those who see a need for change to be patient with others who seem obstinate and closed. It's hard, under pressure, to maintain the unity of the Spirit: to assert our oneness in Christ and work together in harmony toward the one heart and mind that Jesus gives us when we let Him function as our Head.

This is one of the major reasons for this book: to help us in this time of change and challenge to look into the Word to find a basis for unity under pressure and to develop a strategy for approaching differences and tensions between believers that will permit us to come, in God's way, to oneness on the issues that require agreement.

The Bible principles have now been explored. So it's time to think together about applying them to specific cases.

In this chapter, I want to sketch a complex church situation. And then let *you* (after reviewing the first part of the book) plan your own strategy for working out the problems in such a way that unity is reestablished and maintained. The case does *not* describe any particular church, but rather a number of churches—and problems that are in many ways typical. So read the description and work out your own approach to building unity.

MOOREHEAD COMMUNITY CHURCH

It all seemed to happen in the past three years. And really, it was hard to see coming. Suddenly there were these two factions at Moorehead Community Church. There had always been differences, of course. But the board had been harmonious ... too much so, some said, because it always took so long to get down to business ... and in the church the differences in ideas didn't seem that important. Some didn't like the discussion class a new teacher at the junior college had started ...

but others did. So the ones who liked it went there and the others went to old Mr. Karbonski's class to hear him lecture verse by verse.

And the church life went on . . . summer VBS, youth group, choir, many weekday get-togethers as couples and families ate or vacationed together. The church wasn't growing spectacularly, but some were being won to Christ. New families were joining. It was a comfortable church to belong to : . . a good, Bible-believing, Bible-teaching church, a friendly church.

Some thought the change came when Pastor Carl moved* to that church in New Jersey. And the church called the new pastor. Certainly some didn't like his preaching . . . who could have been as good as Pastor Carl? But there were so many other things.

A lot of the members blamed the younger married couples for the problems, especially the "ringleaders" (that bearded Darrel Cotton and the young professor who taught the "discussion" class). Those two were openly critical, talked about the need for more participation in the services, didn't seem to feel that the pulpit ministry was "meeting needs," and read a lot of books that attacked the church and talked about "renewal."

---

*Churches typically change pastors every three to five years. In cases of longer pastorates particularly, a change tends to release tensions and problems that the former man, knowing the people well, had been able to handle or keep submerged. Usually, blaming a new pastor for problems is unfair and unrealistic.

They weren't on the board, of course, but they did seem to influence one or two board members. And *then* they started those "groups!"*

Really, there were three groups. All three met in homes and had only a few members, who seemed enthusiastic and were composed mainly of the younger, more "radical" element. One group soon broke up, but two continued. The members were very excited about learning to "know each other" and about the freedom to "talk over problems." They were struggling with Bible study but finding it hard to keep a focus both on each other and on Scripture. Still, even with that uncertainty, the group members were glowing and told others how much the groups meant to them spiritually.

This report was received with suspicion. What *really* went on in the groups? *Why* was this helping them grow as Christians . . . it didn't seem to fit

---

One of the characteristics of renewal across the country is the development of small sharing groups. Often these are begun apart from sponsorship by the local church and may involve members of the same church or members of various churches. Characteristically there are varying and intense feelings about these groups. To some they are the recovery of New Testament fellowship and vital for Christian growth. To others they seem a threat to the church and an opening of the door to all sorts of excesses and heresy.

There are actually many kinds of "small groups," and they meet for many different purposes. So it is impossible to make a blanket judgment of them. But it is clear that in many churches one great issue that is a cause of conflict is the "small group" issue. For an analysis of small groups in the church, see chapters 12, 13, and 15 of the author's book, A New Face for the Church *(Zondervan, $5.95).*

the traditional pattern of a prayer meeting or a home Bible study. And they met for *hours*—not just for the one hour that marked all church meetings.

So the rumors grew. And the fears. Fear that without an authoritative teacher in the groups, the members wouldn't be able to understand the Bible and would move to some heresy. Fear that they would infect the church or break it up.

The fears grew when the group people kept talking about their experience as something that everyone ought to have (but failed to invite to join them the few who looked on wistfully!). So the issue became one that marked individuals off; people were identified not as "brothers" but as pro- or anti-group. And those against the groups began to question the theological soundness of those in the groups.*

Underlying much of the conflict in such churches today is not a deep-seated theological difference, but, rather, different ideas about "traditional" or "contemporary" expressions of the church's life. The traditionalist tends to view the familiar patterns of church life, the "one way" ministry, and the traditional agencies of the church, as essentially adequate. He also tends to feel that change is threatening, that anyone who wants to change the church is questioning theology and not just present practice or ways of doing.

The "contemporary" often feeds the fears of the traditionalist. He characteristically looks at questioning as an important and valid thing (while the traditionalist deep down feels that this is somehow related to doubting and denying). So the contemporary may raise questions about theological as well as practical issues. This does not necessarily mean he is rejecting traditional theological formulations . . . he is trying to understand

Board meetings and other meetings of church committees became times of conflict. A deep dissatisfaction, with a sense of uncertainty, grew.

After about eight months, the furor over the groups seemed to settle. Groups were still meeting, but their members were also involved in other activities in church. Some taught in the Sunday School, a few were on committees, and while those in the two camps didn't really feel close to each other, neither seemed as suspicious as before.

But the church wasn't growing. In fact, it seemed to be losing ground. And there was a general dissatisfaction and spirit of criticism that kept feelings hurt.

---

them. But to the traditionalist, the very questioning seems like denial.

For this reason, when the traditionalist criticizes or attacks the contemporary, it is nearly always on theological grounds. "He doesn't really believe Scripture is inspired." / "He is rejecting the power of prayer by saying we need group meetings instead of the weekly church prayer meeting." / "He is going to become a heretic if we don't exercise more control over the Bible study when these people meet."

On the other hand, the contemporary is probably very sensitive to interpersonal relationships. His emphasis is on "love one another," and he is trying to rediscover the closeness of fellowship that seems to have marked the Early Church. Often the contemporary is very hurt by the suspicion of the traditionalist. "Doesn't he know me better than that?" / "Doesn't he trust my love for Christ?" And this develops into suspicion on his part . . . suspicion of the motives and love of the traditionalist. Soon he feels he can't be honest with the traditionalist or he will be rejected and defamed. And so the two groups drift apart. Openness in communication breaks down, and they talk primarily about the issue with those in their own camp. The church is polarized and divided.

And then a new issue reared. This time it was over Sunday School. Some began to express a concern that their children (and they) were learning Bible facts, but not how their own lives might be affected.* This was seen by some as a challenge to the doctrine of the divine inspiration of Scripture. Conflict quickly came to a head, centering in the CE and church boards but spilling over throughout the whole church as members took sides.

The quiet that had come when the group issue faded was torn apart by this new issue as scarcely healed wounds were opened, suspicions aroused, and the church once more divided and embroiled in battle.

Unity? Oneness of heart and mind? They were gone, as if they had never existed, and as if they never could exist again.

TYPICAL?

Most churches today have not reached the intense stage of conflict that Moorehead has. But many churches seem to be moving toward it. The two groups, "contemporary" and "traditional," are present in most churches in our country today. In some churches, one group or the other so domi-

---

*This is another issue that is surfacing in many churches. How do we communicate the Word of God . . . to all ages . . . in a life-changing way? Traditional educational settings (the classroom, the student-teacher relationship) are increasingly being probed and criticized, and many today are looking for meaningful modifications of the traditional Sunday School approach . . . ones that provide more help for parents and a greater focus on the home as central in Christian nurture.

110

nates that the minority is submerged, or the few who feel one way or the other move to a church where they are more comfortable.

But as our society and culture change, and particularly as younger adults bring their views and attitudes into our churches, nearly any church can, with startling swiftness, become a Moorehead. The waves of conflict that rise and subside over small groups or Sunday School or something else are symptoms of a division beneath the surface. Even if these particular problems are solved (or ignored), the likelihood is that conflict will develop over less significant things (like length of hair).

If we analyze such conflicts, we'll find:

1. In each battle, the sides will be the same. The division is along "traditional" and "contemporary" lines. If John and Chuck and Bill and Harry are on one side in one issue, probably they'll be on the same side in the next. This alone tells us the battle isn't over the issue itself, that there is something deeper.

2. The conflict will be discussed and fought on theological grounds in evangelical churches. While there may be some theological differences, in most evangelical churches there will be a far more basic agreement on the issues than appears. The conflict actually is rooted in the different persons' approaches to life: their "questioning" or "conservative" attitude.

3. In conflict, communication between the groups diminishes. When there is communication between them, it tends to focus on the problem (and thus

heighten the conflict), rather than involve personal sharing or focus on Christ.

4. There is a frustrating sense of indecision: the feeling that we ought to "do something" but inability to decide what to do. Often this leads to the human solution looked at earlier: the majority tries to pressure the minority to conform. Under this kind of pressure, some leave the church, and there is the danger of a split.

It is, of course, important for our churches to work through questions and issues like those faced by the people of Moorehead. For these are important issues, and we want to know and do God's will in them. But it's important not to let the situation deteriorate as it did at Moorehead. Yet, even in such a disintegrating situation, we *can* rediscover our unity in Christ and live together as Christ's Church, of one heart and of one mind.

QUEST 1

Bible passages to study

Go back over the Scriptures explored in this book, and list them and the principles of unity derived from them.

Go on to complete the form on page 113, which helps you develop a way to reestablish unity at Moorehead.

Personal application

Write out a description of your church (showing ways it is like and/or unlike Moorehead.

Then develop a strategy for strengthening (or reestablishing) unity, using the same form.

A STRATEGY FOR UNITY

I. ANALYSIS (What are the real problems)

II. PRINCIPLES (List Bible principles that apply, as developed in chapters 1-9)

III. PRIORITIES (What do we need to do *first?*)

IV. ACTION IDEAS (How can we achieve our priorities?)

11

Beyond Our Church

A former student of mine, now a Campus Crusade staffer, shared this impression of Explo '72.

The loving, cooperative spirit that pervaded, even through the heat, humidity, and pouring rain, won the hearts of Dallasites. Homes welcomed delegates for lodging or just a visit to share the message of Christ through the Four Spiritual Laws. Literally thousands responded to receive Christ during the week. Can you imagine the thrill of 80,000-plus people cheering as they heard the report of someone receiving Christ? Sounds a little like heaven!

Eighty thousand from all over, from different denominations and associations, loving, cooperating!

We should feel no surprise at something like this. For years organizations such as Youth for Christ, Inter-Varsity, Campus Crusade, and others have drawn young people together and, cutting across denominational and other differences, have worked toward unity. Christian Business Men's Committee and Gideons have worked in the same way with adults. Communitywide evangelistic campaigns have involved members of different churches. Sunday School conventions have opened their doors to all who want to reach others for Christ through improved teaching ministries. We've had "union" Easter services. Ministers have been trained to be pastors of very different churches in the same school . . . such as our largest nondenominational seminary, Dallas Theological.

In many ways we have reached out beyond our own churches and sensed a unity as brothers in Christ, a unity that is deeper and more important than our differences. But probably for most of us this unity is not something personal. Too often our personal contacts with Christians from other groups and backgrounds has remained on the superficial level . . . talking politely, being friendly . . . or it has drifted into talk about our differences, as happened to Bill and his wife (p. 13).

So we wonder. What does unity beyond the local church mean to us? Is there a wider unity that Christians are to seek and to experience?

UNITY

In our thinking about oneness in the Spirit we've uncovered several principles that can be applied in working out our relationships with believers beyond our local church fellowships. We can state these and explore their meaning for us.

Unity is interpersonal, not organizational. Paul encourages, "Be joined together in a brotherhood of mutual love" (Rom. 12:10). While there are many such exhortations to love, and while love is spoken of as the binding force that creates and maintains unity, the New Testament is silent about seeking organizational unity. Instead, it

115

seems to assume that all Christians *are* unified in the Spirit. The divisions it criticizes (such as in 1 Corinthians) are rejected because they involve the formation of factions, in which brother sets himself against brother.

Seeing unity as essentially interpersonal makes such things as drives for "church union" and the organizational merging of denominations not so much wrong as irrelevant. I seek and find my unity with my brother in the fact that we both know and love Christ. Thus we love and seek to build up each other. Our unity is not in the fact that *my* group has merged with *his* group, and we now have the same name on the sign in front of our two churches.

Seeing unity as essentially interpersonal also means that I cannot be satisfied with superficial or organizational unity. This is not an adequate response to Christ's prayer that "they may be one as We are" (John 17:11). Jesus' prayer that *"all* may be one" (John 17:21) specifies that the unity be the same as that which exists between Father and Son. Their unity is organic. It is of nature. It is a unity that *is*, and that is expressed in harmony of purpose and desire, in mutual trust and love and commitment between Father and Son. This is to be the mark of Christian unity: we *are* one in Christ, and oneness is expressed in our harmony of purpose and desire, in our mutual trust and love and commitment to the will of God our Father.

Seeking unity with those outside our local churches, then, must be approached in just the same way as seeking unity within our churches. We need to come to know and love other Christians as persons. Unity means build toward one heart and one mind with them.

God places us in the body. This principle, expressed in 1 Corinthians 12 and other passages, also helps us understand unity. We are not necessarily to rush out seeking unity with believers beyond our local fellowship as though this were some important goal in itself. But we are to become one with those next to whom God places us.

When I was in the Navy, an Army friend and I started a noontime Bible class. Larabee was a Southern Baptist. I (just saved under the ministry of Presbyterian Donald Grey Barnhouse) had joined a GARB [Baptist] church. Conrad, another member of our group, went to a small mission church. And Lee was in a Bible church. But we were all together, there at Brooklyn's New York Port of Embarkation. We all gathered noons to study the Bible, to pray, and to encourage one another.

I didn't seek these people out because they were from different groups and churches. God had put us near each other. So we came together as brothers, literally unaware of our church affiliations.

The other day I went into the office of the company that moved our goods from Illinois to our new home in Phoenix, Ariz. On a table I found a New Testament, with a note from the manager of the company attached. It said that anyone who wished to study the Book was wecome to take it home. I've wondered since. Are there other Christians in that office. Do they find a time to fellow-

117

ship together, to build each other, as our little group did so many years ago in Brooklyn?

They should. *Because when God places members of the body near one another, they are to work toward oneness.* This is the real meaning of unity beyond the local church. We are to build oneness of heart and mind, of love and mutual encouragement, with those near whom God has placed us.

Here we are sensitized to the very practical things we can do to live in accord with Christ's desire that we might "all be one." Is one of our coworkers a believer? Then we need to get to know him or her as a person, to focus our conversations on Christ, to show love and concern, to encourage and build up. Is one of our neighbors a Christian, a member of a different church? We need to build a relationship with that family, to pray together for the unsaved around us, to help each other grow in the Lord. Out of such oneness comes a functioning, working body of Christ, through which Christ, our Head, can direct His redemptive work in our world.

Unity is purposive. God has His reasons for desiring the kind of oneness we've been considering. The first reason has to do with the transforming purpose of the body: that we individually be helped to grow toward Christlikeness. How exciting if every day, in my work, in my neighborhood, I have other Christians to encourage me, other Christians to care about, to pray with, to help me keep my own life focused on Jesus! "I myself am convinced about you, my brothers," Paul wrote to the Romans, "that you are full of goodness, amply furnished with knowledge, and competent to advise

118

one another" (Rom. 15:14). In our experience of oneness with our brothers, we minister to each other in exactly this way.

Unity has another impact: evangelism. Jesus said, "By this everyone will recognize that you are My disciples, if you love one another" (John 13:35). Our love for each other as Christians—not as Baptists or Presbyterians or Methodists or independent Fundamentalists—communicates the reality of Jesus to all around us. It was said of the Early Church, "See how they love one another." The compelling testimony of love caused many to seek out Jesus, the One who alone could so transform men.

Oneness, with its impact on our personal spiritual growth and its demonstration of the reality of different churches to share together in this kind of ministry to the alienated of our communities!

Many organizations began with the gathering of a few Christians for fellowship, who, in response to Christ's leading, reached out in a formal way to meet needs.

While this will happen and—as Christ exercises His perogative to direct the actions of His body—*should* happen in some cases, it is important to keep clearly in mind the fact that organizational unity is secondary to, and an outgrowth of, the unity we find with others in the fellowship of Jesus.

So we do need to "definitely aim for everything that contributes to one another's peace and development" (Rom. 14:19). We do need to reach out to the Christians whom God has placed near us, to

119

love them, to focus each other's lives on Jesus, and to discover in experience that we are one.

QUEST 1

Bible passages to study
Philippians 1:3-14
How did unity (partnership, fellowship) express itself in this church?
Why does Paul stress love as the burden of his prayer (9-11)?
How do people in fellowship affect each other?
John 17:20-23
What kind of oneness does Christ pray for?
Has the prayer been answered, or is it still to be answered? Explain.
How can we as Christians respond to this expressed desire of the Lord?

QUEST 2

Personal application
Beyond-our-church oneness
Who in your neighborhood or at your place of work do you know to be a Christian?
Briefly describe your relationship with each person just named.
What does this suggest about your own response to Christ's desire for unity in the body?

12

All, Together

For a moment in time the Early Church captured the glow of oneness and all that means to those of us who are, together, Christ's body. It was a moment of rest, a moment of peace before a storm of challenge and persecution. It was a moment that lets us realize that God has more for us in our life together than many of us have experienced as yet.

"The believers all met together and had everything jointly; they sold their property and their belongings, and distributed them to all, as anyone might have need. Daily they frequented the Temple together and ate their meals at home together. So they received nourishment, praising God with happy and sincere hearts, and enjoying the good will of all the people, while daily the Lord added to the group those who were being saved" (Acts 2:44-47).

It was a brief moment.

Outside pressures grew, and under persecution the believers were scattered. Sin appeared within the fellowship: Ananias and Sapphira fell, victims of their own greed and hypocrisy. Gentiles were converted, and the strain of adjustment to believers with different life-styles came. Converted

Pharisees, still warped by legalism, struggled against the freedom to love and be loved and to live by simple faith in Jesus. Disputes arose as Greek-speaking Jews felt they were being treated unfairly by their brethren.

But there was a moment of the ideal.

And more.

There was an outworking in the Early Church of the struggle to *maintain* unity. To meet problems and to differ on issues, yes . . . but to remain one in the Spirit. So the Bible tells us that after long discussion of the basis for accepting Gentiles into the new Church, the Jerusalem brothers reported a solution to the Gentile brothers that seemed good to the apostles, and the elders, and the whole church.

Life is to be like this for us.

Not ideal.

But a constant striving to live together God's way: to maintain unity and to experience oneness.

Often people mistake friendship and lack of tension for unity. Actually, it is relatively easy to maintain a semblance of harmony when relationships are superficial. "He doesn't bother me. I just don't see him any more!" This may be one solution to friction. But it isn't God's. God's way is to *move closer* and *love*.

So the marks of unity are positive rather than negative. It isn't the absence of friction that marks oneness in the Spirit. It is the visible expression of love in action: it is reaching out, caring, being involved.

THE MARKS OF UNITY

In the visible and positive marks of unity seen in the early Christians (Acts 2:44-47, quoted earlier), we have clear standards against which to measure our own churches or our relationships with believers in our families or beyond our local congregations.

Meet together. These Christians wanted to be together. The Bible says they gathered daily and frequented the Temple (the place of worship for the early Jewish Christian church). Getting together to worship God, to share and encourage each other, is still a mark of life, vitality, and unity.

Have all jointly. The Early Church expressed its care for one another in a unique and practical way. Private property meant so little to these men and women, who were experiencing and expressing Jesus' love, that they sold what they had in order to give to others.

The church today is not commanded to the communal life by this example. No other passages of Scripture teach this; instead, the right of private property is upheld (cf. Acts 5:4; 1 Cor. 16:2; 1 Tim. 6:17-19). What is exhorted is a practical expression of the love that cements us together as one. *We are to care for one another.* Such love for each other holds material possessions unimportant in comparison to a brother's welfare (cf. 1 John 3:17, 18). Thus the New Testament pattern for giving, expressed in 2 Corinthians 8, 9, which supersedes the Old Testament ties, exhorts us to share whatever we have that our brothers' needs might be met and that we might together thank God for His supply.

Today we can say this mark of oneness, not in charity, but in the spontaneous reaching out of believer to believer to share what God has given—naturalness and joy. When we love one another so that persons count more than what we possess, then we have visible evidence of oneness in the Spirit.

Eat together. Just as gathering daily in the Temple indicates how love drew the believers together for congregational worship and encouragement, their daily eating of their "meals at home together" shows how love drew them together informally as well. These people found the person of Jesus Christ an exciting bond. They loved to be with each other.

The New Testament puts much emphasis on hospitality. Why? Because being together in informal settings, meeting as friends, eating together, sitting around a home evenings sharing . . . these things build and stimulate love. We come to know and care about those with whom we spend time. When we have Jesus in common as a bond and see Him at work in each other's lives, we have one of the most powerful stimulants to spiritual growth.

Where oneness is, Christians seek out each other's company and love to be with one another.

Praise God. It's important to note that the praising of God that the Acts passage mentions takes place in the context of the home and the meal. This is no formal church service. This is an example of the *focus on Jesus* that marks the conversation and the contact of brothers and sisters.

When Jesus is acting in our lives, when we share

with each other what He means to us and is doing in us, praise is spontaneous. The people who are experiencing oneness and that unity the Bible invites us all to know will be marked by just this joy and praise.

Happy and sincere hearts. "Sincere" in the Bible is "unhypocritical," without phoniness or fraud. These believers found the freedom in Christ to be real with one another . . . to open their hearts and "speak truth each man with his neighbor."

Openness and honesty in our relationships with brothers is another mark of unity. When we are free to be ourselves, when we live this way with each other, we experience the happiness that only acceptance and forgiveness can bring.

Good will of all. A striking result of the joyous fellowship of the Early Church was the good will of those around. Somehow people were unable to criticize or attack the brothers, who radiated love and cared for each other so intensely. Love is hard to hate. We can be hated for our doctrine (in our pluralistic society the insistence on Jesus as only Saviour and commitment to Scripture as His authoritative Word are likely to bring quick opposition!). But it is hard to be hated for loving.

This isn't to say that Christian unity wards off all persecution and criticism. It does not. A world that hated Christ will hardly love His disciples.

It *is* to say, however, that if we are living in unity and love, the antagonism of the world will not be aroused by *us*. It's tragic that so often people reject Jesus without a hearing because of the lives of Christians. When we love one another and thus grow in our capacity to love everyone, we have a chance to get close enough to non-Christians so that the issue can be Jesus . . . not our failings or faults. We need this evidence of unity in our churches and in our communities.

Adding to the group. The Bible tells us that daily the Lord added to the Church those who were being saved. How striking that effective evangelism is also a mark of unity and oneness in the Spirit!

The song says, "And they'll know we are Christians by our love." We can go beyond this. They will come to know our Saviour and be added to his church when we love.

Where there is oneness in the Spirit there is growth through evangelism. For Christian love is not exclusive. Instead, it reaches out beyond our group to other people and seeks to draw them to Jesus. When we know the love of God within our fellowship, that same love overflows compellingly to others.

We can, then, measure objectively the oneness we know, or fail to know, in our churches and fellowships. The measures are these: Where there is oneness in the Spirit, there will be . . .

1. Meeting together for worship and encouragement as congregations.

2. An attitude between brothers that "what is mine is yours."

3. Meeting together informally in homes.

4. A focus in formal and informal gatherings on Jesus and what He is doing in our lives . . . with resultant praise and joy.

5. Sincerity and honesty in our relationships.

6. The good will of those outside Christ for us as persons.

7. An effective evangelism that sees others being won to Christ regularly.

These marks constitute, together, objective evidence of the oneness of the Spirit.

WON FOR US

It is easy, in looking at the marks of unity and comparing our own situations, to become discouraged. I suppose that in many ways all of us fall short of the ideal.

But we need not be discouraged.

Why?

Because Jesus Christ on Calvary has won unity for us. We are *one* in the Spirit.

This is where our book began—with an assertion of this basic Bible truth: we *are* one. We are brothers and sisters in Christ.

We have then no impossible task, and we dream no impossible dream in seeking to experience oneness. We are not called on to create something from nothing or to change reality. Instead, we are invited by God to experience something that He says does exist and is real.

As we've seen, Jesus hasn't left us ignorant of how to experience unity. We start with a realization of who we are. And of what we are to each other. We move on by reaching out to know one another in love . . . to know our brothers and sisters as Christ knows them. As love grows, as we learn to care for each other in practical ways, those irrelevant differences that have divided us recede in importance. We focus our relationship around the Person and will of our common Lord. And we grow in our ability to sense, as a responsive body, His will.

This unity is ours to claim.

Unity is ours to maintain and to build by reaching out to each other with Jesus' own love.

And so, understanding God's will for His Church that we may be one, even as Jesus and the Father are one, we are freed to respond with joy and thankfulness. Jesus has reconciled us . . . to God, and to one another.

Let us live together in unity.

Let us begin to love.

QUEST

Personal application

   What have I done during this study to reach out to others in love?

   With whom have I sought to establish and maintain oneness?

   What principles have been most difficult for me to understand and apply?

   What principles have been most important to me?

   What would God have me to do now?